INTRODUCTION TO THE ORIGINAL EXCEL SAGA VOL. 1:

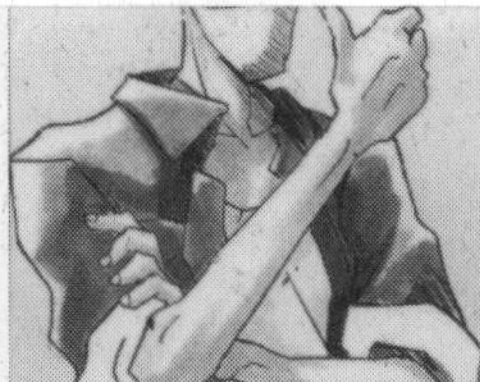

AUTHOR
Rikdo Koshi

"Nice to meet you. I'm Rikdo Koshi, here with my first compilation. I hope you'll look forward to reading my work in the future."

FURRY ARTISAN
Genkotsu #2

"Heh! You lucked out big time, didn't ya. C'mon, draw some more furries--more furries, damn it."

"My, if it isn't dear Genkotsu #2, dropout from the human race. This place is not for you --do you understand?"

"You're one to talk. Hey, there's still time. Come on over to this side... where I am."

"Ha-ha, listen to the fool spout nonsense. What is this side that you refer to?"

"It's...ohhhh, such a wonderful place..."

(According to these comments, it would appear that Rikdo Koshi and Genkotsu #2 are in fact different people.)

INTRODUCTION TO THE ENGLISH EXCEL SAGA VOL. 1:

This work deals with the everyday aspects of living in Japan, so there might be a fair number of things that may seem puzzling.

While the story's locale is based on a certain regional city in Japan, Excel is in fact a hard-working and strongly motivated woman of the kind you could find anywhere.

The only thing is, her goals are all screwed up. I hope those of you in America will find this dedicated and straightforward protagonist to be likeable.

—Rikdo Koshi, March 2003

STORY AND ART BY
RIKDO KOSHI

EXCEL SAGA 01

STORY AND ART BY
RIKDO KOSHI

ENGLISH ADAPTATION BY
DAN KANEMITSU & CARL GUSTAV HORN

TRANSLATION
DAN KANEMITSU

LETTERING & TOUCH-UP BY
BRUCE LEWIS & CARL GUSTAV HORN

GRAPHIC DESIGN
BRUCE LEWIS

LAYOUT ASSISTANCE
JOSH KEILER & CAROLINA UGALDE

EDITOR
CARL GUSTAV HORN

EDITOR IN CHIEF, BOOKS
ALVIN LU

EDITOR IN CHIEF, MAGAZINES
MARC WEIDENBAUM

VP OF PUBLISHING LICENSING
RIKA INOUYE

VP OF SALES
GONZALO FERREYRA

SR. VP OF MARKETING
LIZA COPPOLA

PUBLISHER
HYOE NARITA

Printed in Canada.

Published by VIZ Media, LLC
P.O. Box 77064
San Francisco, CA 94107

VIZ Media Edition
10 9 8 7
First printing, July 2003
Seventh printing, March 2007

THIS WORLD...!
...IS CORRUPT!
DUM DUM DUM DUM DE-DUM DUM DE-DU
(HOW IS IT CORRUPT? FOR THE MOMENT, WE SHALL DECLINE TO ELABORATE!)
THIS GLOBE IN ITS ENTIRETY MUST BE SET ARIGHT... AND YET!
SHOULD SUDDENLY THE WORLD BECOME UNIFIED UNDER MY RULE--I DOUBT NOT THAT THE IGNORANT MASSES SHALL BE LAGGARD!
THEREFORE, WHY NOT JUST A SINGLE NATION?
BUT THEN, TO AVOID OVERSTRETCH -- WHY NOT GO ONE STEP BEYOND?
NOW THERE IS NO TREPIDATION!
A PRUDENT FIRST STAGE TO WORLD DOMINATION!
IN OTHER WORDS, OUR GOAL IS...

THE CONQUEST OF THIS CITY!

FWOONT

MMP

THHHWUMMP

MISSION 1
THE INITIATION OF A LEGEND
HAIL IL PALAZZO!

YES! THIS IS A CERTAIN CITY IN A CERTAIN PREFECTURE...

...or rather somewhere BENEATH that city...
THE PEOPLE CANNOT EVEN SAVE THEIR OWN PERSONS...

...secretly, the HEADQUARTERS of the super-secret syndicate ACROSS!
...LET ALONE THE MASSES AS A BODY...
YOU ARE AB-SO-LUTE-LY RIGHT!

...an organization attempting to conquer THIS CITY -- as ONE STEP towards... the WHOLE WORLD!

WE MUST LET IT BE KNOWN THAT ONLY WE CAN LEAD THE WORLD TO...
LORD IL-PAL-LAZ-ZO! ÜB-ER AL-LES!
PUHPRRRRHHHT
KLAKLLAK KLAK

..IT, UH, ALL MEANS THAT...
DUM DE DUM DE DUM
KA KLAK KA KLAK
UNH! UNH! FOR YOU, I, EXCEL, WILL JUMP INTO FIRE OR WATER...!

KYAAAAAAAAAAAAAA
YOINK
KACHNNNK
PLOOSH
LET'S HAVE YOU DO *THAT*, THEN.

UMM... *SIR?* LORD *IL PALAZZO?*
KAF
KOF
WHEEZE
FURTHERMORE, WE MERELY STRIVE TO MAKE THAT *FIRST* STEP...
SIR?
SIR?

OUR MISSION IS A *LONG* AND *TORTUROUS* PATH...
...THAT EVEN THE *GREAT MEN* OF YESTERYEAR WERE NOT ABLE TO ACCOMPLISH...

HAK
WHAT *IS* IT, EXCEL?
UH, WHAT'S WITH THE *PIT*, SIR?
UMM, *YES*...
WHEEZE
GASP

PULL TO PURGE ENEMIES
PLASH
AIEEEEEE!
I CAN'T TOUCH BOTTOM!
PLOSH
I CAN'T TOUCH BOTTOM!
PADDLE PADDLE PADDLE

WAS IT TOO *SHALLOW?*
SHAKETYSHAKETYSHAKE
plish
plish
plish

EXCEL, WOULD YOU MIND IF I ASKED YOU A *QUESTION?*
NO SIR!

WHAT IS THE *MEANING* OF THAT *DOLL* YOU POSSESS TODAY?

THANK YOU FOR ASKING!

KTHMPT

DA-DMMPT

WITH OUR AIM OF CONQUERING THIS CITY, ACROSS (THE ORGANIZATION FOR THE PROMOTION OF THE INSTITUTIONALIZATION OF THE [SUPREME IDEOLOGICAL] IDEAL [ON EARTH]) ADHERING TO THE PRINCIPLE OF BEING THOSE FEW AND SELECT -- CONSISTS OF OUR GREAT LEADER LORD IL PALAZZO...
...AND MYSELF, MULTITASKING AS EXECUTIVE OFFICER, STAFF OFFICER, COMBATANT, LATRINE ORDERLY, AND SO ON -- WITH A GRAND TOTAL MEMBERSHIP OF TWO...
...BUT -- FEELING THIS WAS TOO SCANTY A ROSTER, INVESTED ¥2500* (OF MY OWN MONEY) FOR PARTS, AND, PULLING AN ALL-NIGHTER...
¥2500*= US $20.83 -- CGH

HUP
...CARVED THIS OUT.
NAME: DUMMY
I SEE...

I SHALL HASTEN TO ALLEVIATE THE HUMAN RESOURCES PREDICAMENT.
OH, LORD IL PALAZZO!... THAT'S SO...

...I HAD NO IDEA...
TO IMAGINE THAT I HAD BEEN FORCING SUCH HARDSHIPS UPON YOU, EXCEL...

IN THE MEANTIME, THE DOLL SHALL SERVE AS EXECUTIVE OFFICER, AND YOU, EXCEL, SHALL RETAIN THE DESIGNATION OF COMBATANT AND LATRINE ORDERLY.
LET'S TORCH THIS PIECE OF GARBAGE.
HUP
CHIK
FWOOMMMP

NOW, REGARDING TODAY'S PLANS...
POP
CRIKL
SNAP
SZZZ

WOOPS...
POOF

EXTINGUISH THE FIRE.
...THE SWEET P'TATERS ARE ALMOST DONE...
BUUUUT...
POP

FWOMP
HUP
HUP
STOMPITY
STOMPITY

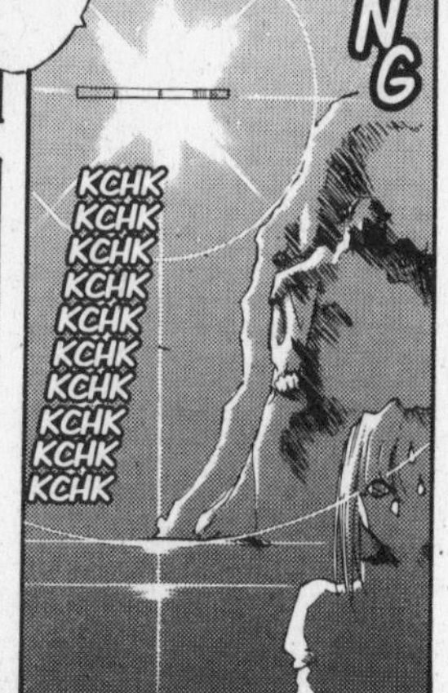
NOW, WE HAVE THIS FILM FOOTAGE ...
KCHUNNNG
KCHK KCHK KCHK KCHK KCHK KCHK KCHK KCHK KCHK KCHK

KCHK KCHK KCHK KCHK KCHK KCHK KCHK KCHK
OH WOW. THIS LOOKS SO COOL...
1

!
creeeeeeek
hobble
BUP

AN... OLD HAG ?
WOW, SHE'S LIKE SKIN AND BONES...
THAT WOULD BE AN ELDERLY WOMAN.
CHIKA CHIKA CHIKA CHIKA

NOW -- WE HAVE HERE AN ELDERLY WOMAN THAT LOOKS HARMLESS, BUT, IN FACT ...
BREE BREE BREE
OH! MY PHONE!

Be Beep
YES, HELLO, IT'S ME . . .
......
WHAT? RIGHT NOW?
NO, THAT'S FINE.
YES, I'LL BE RIGHT OVER.
YES SIR!

UM, THAT BEING THE CASE...
...I NEED TO GO TO MY PART-TIME JOB NOW...
YOU POSSESS SUCH A RUDE OBJECT AS A CELL PHONE?
KLIK
FWUUMP

SURPRISING THAT IT DID NOT BREAK AFTER BEING SUBMERGED...
HEH HEH! IT'S WATERPROOF!
KA-POSE

THAT WILL BE COMFORTING.
AUGH!
CRROAK CRROAK CRROAK
CRROAK
CRROAK CRROAK
CRROAK
CRROAK
CRROAK
CRROAK CRROAK
TOADS?!?
WHY TOADS ?!?
AIEEEEEE!

CRROAK
CRROAK
WELL, I'LL BE ON MY WAY NOW...
SPLASH PADDLE SPLISH PLASH
SHFF SHFF

BEEP BOOP BOMP BEEP BEEP BEEP BEEP
RRRRRRRRRRRRR
HELLO. WOULD THIS BE THE OFFICES OF HISHI JAPAN NEWSPAPERS?
PLOSH PLOOSH
WAAAAH!

I'D LIKE TO PLACE A HELP-WANTED AD...
VRRRRRRRRRNNNN
HONNNK
KTHUNK KTHUNK KTHUNK
NSTRUCTION
ATER MAIN
NE 30 / JULY 4
PAN HIGHWAY CONSTRUCTION CORP
YAMURA DOKEN CONSTRUCTION INC
HONNNK
BEEEEP
HUH?
OH, ME?
VRRRRRRRRRRRN
KLANNG KLANNG

HEY, YOU! STOP!
STOP RIGHT THERE!
OKAY, GREEN LIGHT!
SSSHINNG
OKAY, LET'S KEEP IT MOVING! KEEP IT MOVING!
TWIRL TWIRL
FWEET FWEET

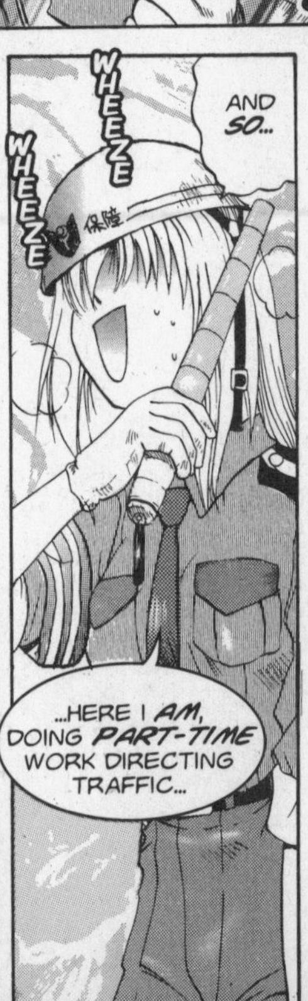
WHEEZE
WHEEZE
AND SO...
...HERE I AM, DOING PART-TIME WORK DIRECTING TRAFFIC...

HUFF PUFF
YAY!
YAY!
IN FACT, THIS JOB PAYS PRETTY WELL...
HEY THERE, LADY. YOU SURE LIKE TALKING TO YOURSELF, DON'T 'CHA?

RMMMMMMMMMMMMMMMMM
'ELLO! MISTER FOREMAN!
CAN I HELP YOU?!
AH...
SSHING

TEN TON TRUCK COMIN' IN.
VRRRMM
...HUMMPT
AACK

YOU ALL RIGHT?
FH-FHHAD TH-THAT 'US ARRIDLE WAS A LITTLE SHKEREEE... SCARY...
OOH OHH
...got a nice present, right smack into my nose...

...everyone on the site is so nice...
WHSSH WHSSH
KANGG KaNNGG
RATTLE RATTLE
KEEPIN' UP, GAL?
...when you think about it, these are the people building new parts of the city that will eventually belong to us...
...so it's only natural that I be magnanimous toward them...
HONNNK
BEEEEEP

There are those inconsiderate drivers that don't stop, but...
VRMMMM

...I almost feel sorry for them as I jot down their license plate numbers for the coming purge...
the litty bitty blacklist

...from middle-aged men...
...to office ladies...
...yes, even little doggies!
why not?
woof

EVERYBODY AND EVERYTHING WILL ONE DAY BE OUR SLAVES!...

...YOU MUST CONQUER THE WORLD SOON, LORD IL PALAZZO!

HAHAHA...

I THOUGHT I'D SAID THAT THERE'S A LONG ROAD AHEAD OF US...

OH, I'M SORRY, BUT I JUST CAN'T KEEP IT INSIDE ME!

WHRRRLL

WHRRL

TWIRL

HAHHH HAHHH WHRRRL

THUD
SKREEEREEECH
SKRESH
BANG

WHAT *IS* IT?
MAJOR *CAR CRASH!*

CALL AN *AMBULANCE!*
GET THAT *FIRE* OUT!

THIS IS HORRIBLE!
I -- I CAN'T GET THE DOOR OPEN!
ARE YOU ALIVE?

MY CHILDREN! MY CHILRDEN ARE INSIDE!
MY *ARM! MY ARRRRRM!*

...a conspiracy! this must be some sort of conspiracy!

mr. foreman... and everyone else on this site -- i'm so sorry you all got mixed up in this!

...but i sure am glad i used a fake name on the w-4...

please help me, lord il palazzo...!

オオオオ

...HM.
GOOD.

VOID
city conquest base plan #1023
city conquest base plan #1024

WHY NOT TAKE A MOMENT TO RELAX?

HELLO, YES. I WOULD LIKE A DELIVERY TO BE MADE.
HM, YES. THE "GERMAN DELUXE" PIZZA TICKLES MY FANCY...
WHAT?
MY ADDRESS?
MY PHONE NUMBER?

I HAVE NO TONGUE THAT COULD UTTER SUCH TO ONE AS MENIAL AS YOU!

I'M HOOOME!

HEY! WELCOME HOME!

HEY, THERE'S SOMETHING I'M JUST DYING TO TELL YOU! I HAD A TERRIBLE DAY TODAY!
OH, THAT'S TOO BAD. WELL, HEY, JUST SIT BACK AND RELAX!

...I KNOW, LORD IL PALAZZO, I KNOW...
"Even if I cough, I am alone..."
TALKING TO YOURSELF IS NOT GOOD.
1

ガチャ
SIGH

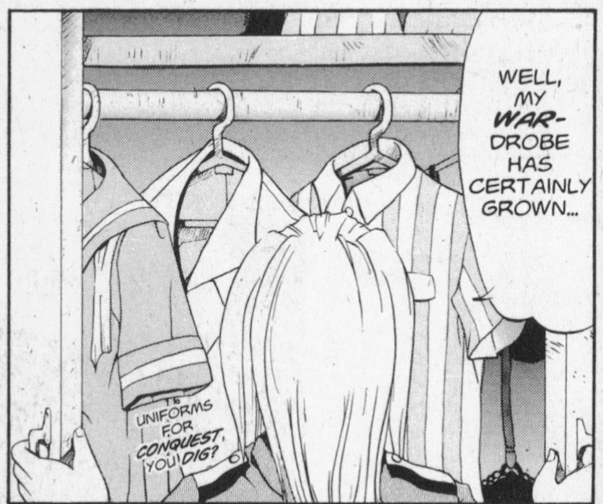
WELL, MY WARDROBE HAS CERTAINLY GROWN...
UNIFORMS FOR CONQUEST, YOU DIG?

i realize that world unificatio will incite acts of terror from the ignorant masses, but...
...they're all so devious about making it look like I did it...
...and i was actually able to keep going for two whole weeks on the last job...
IST

...but who would do such a horrible act as the one today?..

SHE'S ALREADY REWRITTEN HER MEMORY OF THE INCIDENT.

OH, WELL-- WHAT'S PAST IS *PAST!* GOTTA LOOK TOWARDS THE *FUTURE!*

TIME TO GO TO *SLEEP!*

GOOD NIGHT!

......

what about that old hag I saw at headquarters today?
lord il palazzo, what was it you wanted to say...?

...some guerrilla fighter?
is this the I-RRRRR-A?
no, that couldn't...
...no, that must be it!

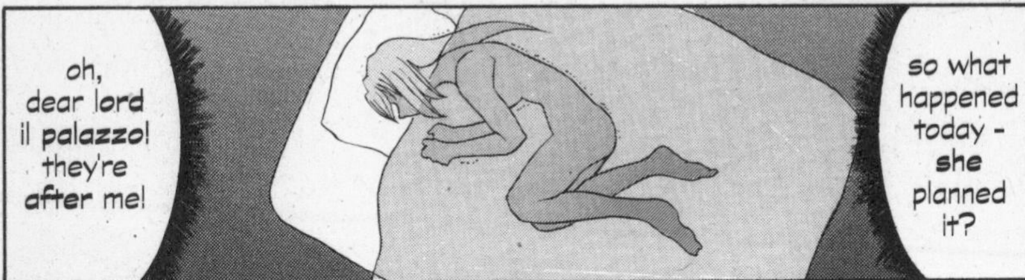
so what happened today - she planned it?
oh, dear lord il palazzo! they're after me!

help - !
Z
スャ
スャ
スャ

...PRETTY PATHETIC...
キン

THE HAG!

THE OLD HAG IS-!

THE OLD HAAAAG!

THE ELDERLY WOMAAAAN!

WHATEVER!

ENOUGH...

...ABOUT THE OLD HAG!

DIE, OLD HAG! DIE!
I WON'T GO DOWN ALO
HURRAY FOR ACROSS
DAMNIT, I SHOULD HAVE KNOWN SOMETHING LIKE THIS MIGHT HAPPEN...
...CONSDERING HOW LITTLE THEY WANTED FOR THE SECURITY DEPOSIT..
WHO THE HELL IS LIVING NEXT DOOR?
OWWoOOOOOOOOO
Frstle Frstle Frstle
GOOD MORNING, LORD IL PALAZZO!
IF YOU DON'T MIND, I HAVE A QUESTION TO ASK...
UM...
...WHAT WAS THE DEAL WITH THE FOOTAGE OF THE ELDERLY WOMAN YESTERDAY?

END MISSION 1

"Reveal anything, and I go down the hatch. So sorry..."

Featured Character #1

ACROSS

The Organization for the Promotion of the Institutionalization of the [Supreme Ideological] Ideal [On Earth]

THE SEVEN SECRETS OF

EXCEL

(CODENAME)

- Her name is a mystery
- Her age is a mystery
- Her birthplace and where she grew up are mysteries
- That strange outfit is certainly a mystery
- Everything about her past and how she came to be is a mystery
- It's also a mystery how someone as incompetent as her got to be the protagonist
- How she climbs out of that trapdoor chute is a real mystery
- It's completely mysterious how she came to belong to ACROSS
- Crap... we got eight mysteries!
- I wonder if they saw this coming

Featured Character #2

ACROSS

The Organization for the Promotion of the Institutionalization of the [Supreme Ideological] Ideal [On Earth]

THE GREAT LEADER

IL PALAZZO

(HIS SECRETS)

"Secrecy is the art of covertly hiding unbeknownst information from people."

...or so he claims.

this year's rainy season is rather extended...
...but i actually don't mind the season that much.
...a nice umbrella and raincoat...
snails and hydrangeas ...
...doesn't it feel a little bit like a storybook fairy tale?
yet, what with this weather...

MISSION 2
TODAY AND TOMORROW FOR FAREWELLS

WELL, WELL...

TO *THINK* THAT AN *UNDERGROUND HEADQUARTERS* WOULD POSSESS SUCH A *WEAKNESS...*
...IT WAS SOMETHING I HAD NOT *FORESEEN.*

UGM ...
WHAT DO *YOU* MAKE OF THIS SITUATION, *EXCEL?*
UGM... *WYEATH!*

WELL, SIR, IN ORDER TO KINDLE SOME FAINT SEMBLANCE OF *HOPE* AMIDST THESE *DIRE CIRCUMSTANCES,* I FELT EAGER -- EVEN COMPELLED -- TO SEND SOME *DECOYS* FLOATNG FORTH...
got lightheaded for a moment
YOU CERTAINLY ARE *FOND* OF THOSE THINGS, *AREN'T* YOU?

IN ANY CASE... FROM LEFT TO RIGHT: EXECUTIVE OFFICER, STAFF OFFICER, COMBATANT—AND YOU, EXCEL, AS LATRINE ORDERLY.
PLEASE, SIR, LET'S RECRUIT MORE PEOPLE BEFORE WE ASSIGN STAFF POSITIONS TO INORGANIC OBJECTS.
GOSH... ISN'T THAT THE NAME OF A FAMOUS SUMO WRESTLER FROM THE EDO PERIOD?
boy, lord il palazzo sure is cultured!
TO ME, THEY CONJURE THE GHASTLY IMAGE OF THE BLOATED CORPSE OF DOZAEMON.
MOVING ON, THEN...
...WE WILL NOW BEGIN DELIBERATION OF TODAY'S CITY CONQUEST PLAN, # 1154.
TELL ME, EXCEL—WHAT WOULD YOU REGARD AS AN INTEGRAL COMPONENT OF CHILDRENS' EDUCATION?
SIR?
WELL, UM...
UM... LET'S SEE...
I GUESS... THE HEART MIGHT BE IMPORTANT?
HMM...
MIND CONTROL for all good brats CHILLUNS

CHILDREN WITH *ENRICHED HEARTS* WILL BECOME *ENLIGHTENED CITIZENS*...

..*ENLIGHTENED CITIZENS* WILL UNDOUBTEDLY ACCEPT THE RULERSHIP OF THE *RIGHTEOUS LEADER.*

ANY IDEAS ON *SPECIFIC STEPS* TO BE TAKEN TO ENRICH THE HEARTS OF CHILDREN?

SIR!

GO AHEAD.
SIR! ENRICHED *HEARTS* FROM ENRICHED *MEALS!*
I HUMBLY SUGGEST— SHALL WE NOT ATTEMPT TO IMPROVE THE QUALITY OF THE HOT SCHOOL LUNCH?!?

WAS IT... A... BAD IDEA?
NO, I DO NOT THINK IT IS A BAD IDEA...

DO YOU NOT THINK RATHER THAT IT IS AN IMPOSSIBLE IDEA?
YES. I REALIZE THAT IT WAS MY SUGGESTION... YET -- SOMEHOW -- I FIND THAT I MUST CONCUR.
school can't even make curry taste good...

MOVING ON TO THE NEXT PLAN...
HM?

LORD IL PALAZZO, IT'S TIME FOR ME TO GO TO WORRRKK...
......

DON'T YOU FEEL...

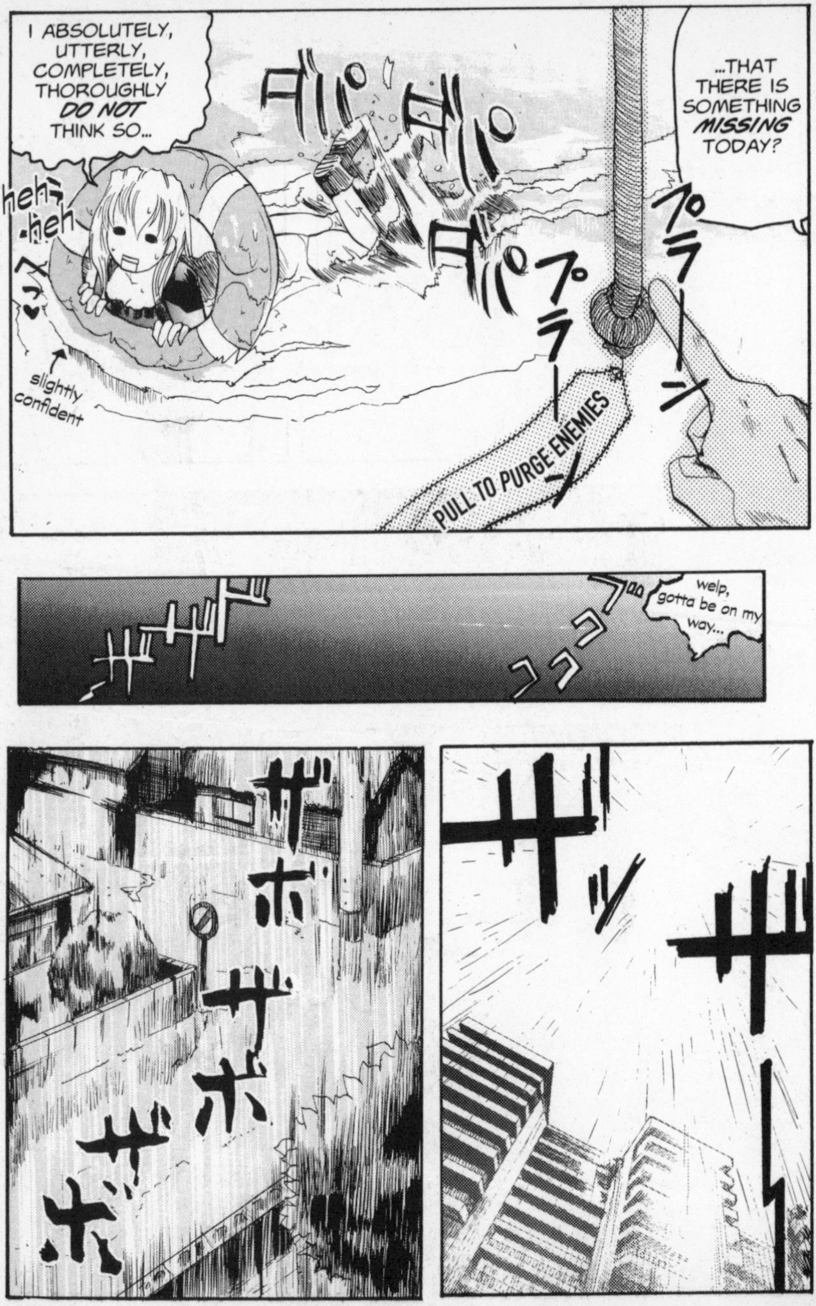

...THAT THERE IS SOMETHING *MISSING* TODAY?

I ABSOLUTELY, UTTERLY, COMPLETELY, THOROUGHLY *DO NOT* THINK SO...

heh heh

slightly confident

PULL TO PURGE ENEMIES

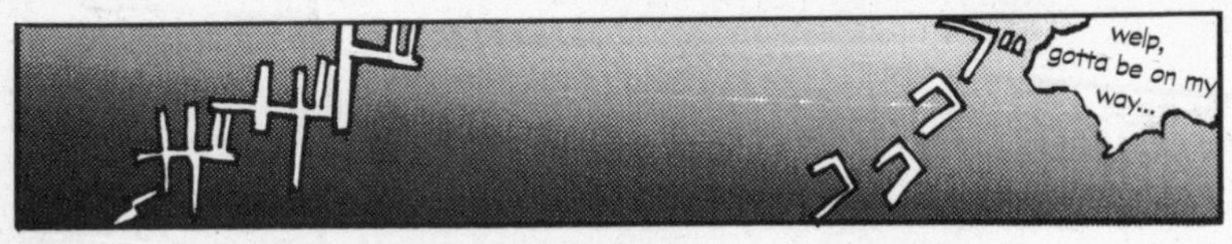

DO YOU KNOW... WHAT MY NAME IS...
it's actually a se-cret.
...IT'S ALREADY BEEN THREE DAYS FOR ME ON THE EVENING DELIVERY RUN...
JUST THREE DAYS...
...AND ALREADY I'M IN AN EMERGENCY SITUATION LIKE THIS...
this ain't no overflow unoff... it's a bona fide flood

OKAY WOW.
JUST LOOK AT ALL THE STUFF THAT'S FLOATING ABOUT...

LOOKS LIKE THE COLONEL'S MAKING A DELIVERY DOWN TO DAVY JONES'S LOCKER...

...AND OVER THERE, A PUPPY BEING WASHED AWAY...
YELP! YAP! HYAP!

PUPPY?

Dog
Organism
EDIBLE

MM HMM!

AH-HA HA HA!
ギャン!
ギャフッ
KIDDING! I'M ONLY KIDDING! ...

I MEAN, I HARDLY EVER GET HUNGRY ENOUGH TO EAT A DOG!*
いやあああ
ポタ
ポタ

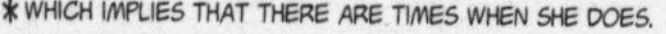
* WHICH IMPLIES THAT THERE ARE TIMES WHEN SHE DOES.

AWW... I'LL GIVE YOU A NICE *TREAT* WHEN I'M DONE WORKING...
ザブ
ザブ

♪ ♫
BI-*CYC*-LE! BI-*CYC*-LE!
♪ ♫
BI—

ざー…
HUH?

gone in sixty seconds... or maybe less!
"stolen"?
stolen — with the finesse of a cat burglar!

...and almost certainly by a state-sponsored conspiracy!
but... it isn't stolen...

BUT DON'T WORRY, PUPPY!
I SHALL NOT BE DEFEATED!

WITH DAWN OVER A CONQUERED CITY FAST APPROACHING...
...I CANNOT LET SOME pettybicyclethief STATE CONSPIRACY DEFEAT ME NOW!

HA HA HA HA HA HA

I'M HO-OHME!
THANK GOD THE WATER HASN'T REACHED HERE YET...
I'LL BET THE PUPPY IS TIRED, TOO...
心労
CAN'T KEEP CALLIN YOU "PUPP THOUGH... GOT GIVE YOU A NAME...
aieeeeeeee
HMM...
RIGHT. "MINCE!"
YOUR NAME IS MINCE!
MMM... DOESN'T IT JUST SOUND SO FATTY, CHEAP AND TASTY...?
PROSPECT-OF-BEING-EATEN-O-GRAPH
%
ODDS
ELAPSED TIME
whiiinne
SSSSSSSSS
SOUND OF HOLE BURNING THROUGH MINCE'S STOMACH.
ALL RIGHT THEN.
TIME FOR FOOD!
%
ODDS
ELAPSED TIME

AHH! MINCE!
AIEEEEE
BAD! BAD MINCE!
WHAT? WHAT IS IT?
C'MON, NO MORE BAD
SHUT UP!
I'VE HAD ENOUGH OF THIS CRAP!
the

ガチャッ
YOU... DAMN... HUH?
THIS HAS GOTTA BE DRIVING YOU CRAZY, TOO! GO AHEAD AND LET IT OUT!
ズカズカ
ズカズカ
HEY-- YOU'RE THE GUY THAT LIVES NEXT DOOR!
YOU'RE THE ONE...
THAT'S TOO... FRICKIN'... LOUD!
ゴオ
YIKES!

NO, I'M NOT THE--
SHUT UP! YOU'RE THE ONE THAT'S ALWAYS LETTING OUT THOSE WEIRD SCREAMS!
I SAID I'M NOT THE ONE WHO'S DOIN' IT, DAMMIT!
IT SURE IS A SCARY WORLD, HUH? ROUGH AND TOUGH OUT THERE...
RIGHT?
i give up...

HEY, MY CELL PHONE ...

YES, WHO IS IT? OH, LORD IL PALAZZO! YES? WHAT CAN I DO FOR YOU...?
ACK
OH, THE NOISE? PLEASE DON'T LET IT BOTHER YOU...
UCK
HEY, IT STOPPED
YES?... RIGHT NOW?... I UNDERSTAND, SIR.... ...I'LL BE THERE QUICKLY...!

HUH?

WHAT WAS IT? SOUNDED LIKE SOMEONE DUMPING THEIR TRASH ON THE GROUND...

PEOPLE REALLY NEED TO BE MORE *CIVIC-MINDED.*

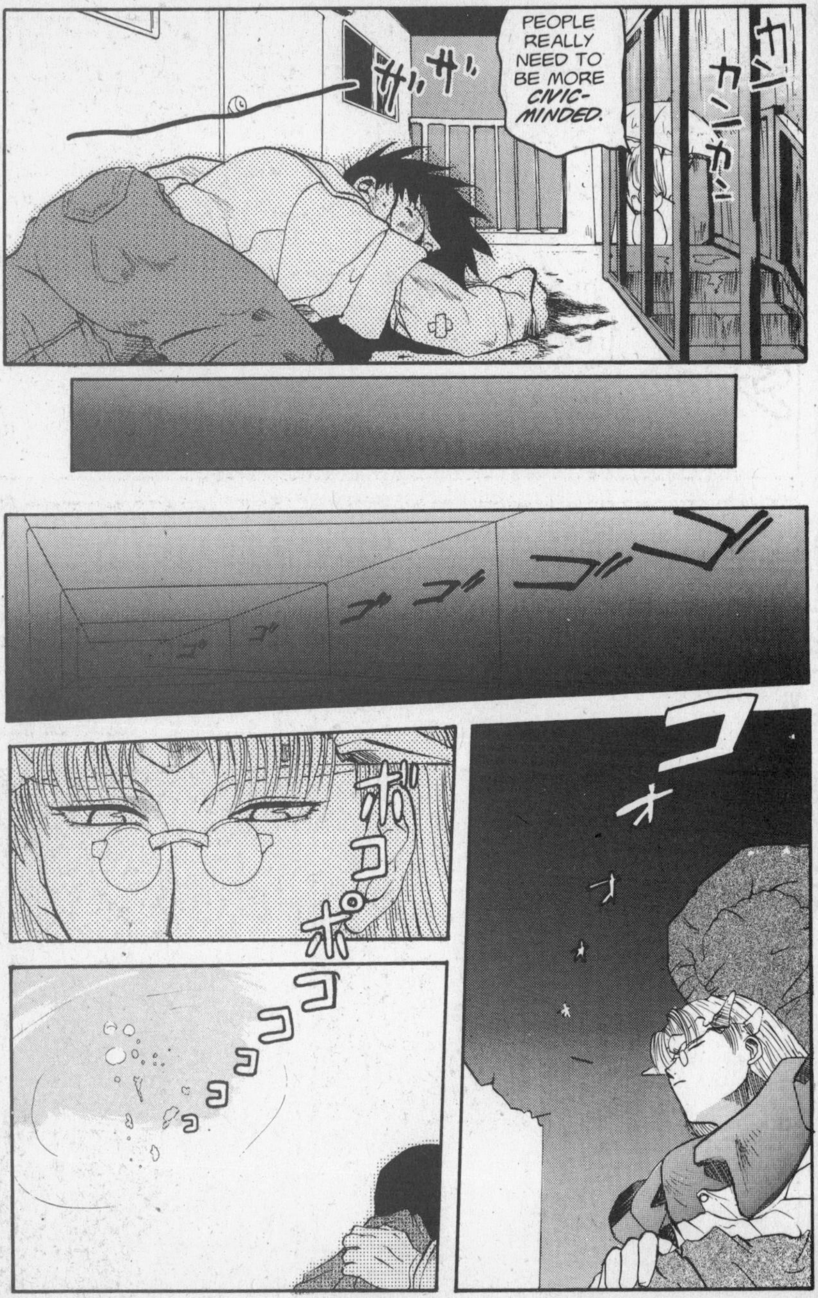

PFFFUT
ズッ
ヤ
ポ
ポッ
ポペン

THAT WAS QUITE FAST.
HAIL
IL
PALAZZO
ゲボッ
ブル
ブル
プルン
チャプン

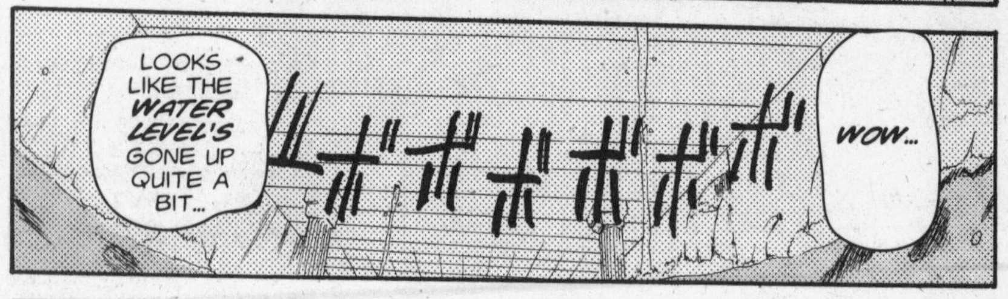

WOW...
LOOKS LIKE THE WATER LEVEL'S GONE UP QUITE A BIT...
ボボボボボボ

WHY DON'T WE DO SOMETHING, LORD IL PALAZZO?
YES, WE CERTAINLY MUST DO SOMETHING...

BY THE WAY, WHY IS THERE A DOG ON YOUR HEAD?
OH, I JUST FOUND HER.
HER NAME IS MINCE...
チャプン
キャプン

SIR, WHY DON'T WE GO AHEAD AND HAVE HER BE AN ACROSS COMBATANT?
--AND EXECUTIVE OFFICER, AND STAFF OFFICER, AND HAVE YOU BE THE LATRINE ORDERLY?

ACK!

UM, OUR SECRET ACROSS HEADQUARTERS... ...IT IS EQUIPPED WITH A BATHROOM, ISN'T IT?
YES, WHAT ABOUT IT?

I'M THINKING... THIS BATHROOM MUST BE MESSED UP BAD, WHAT WITH ALL THIS FLOODING...
AND NOT ONLY DID I SWIM IN THIS, BUT I DRANK SOME OF THIS...
...must-use-proper-syntax...!
AND... REAL TENSE SITUATION THIS... UM, IS... AND...

WHOOOOAAAAAAAAAAAAAAAAAAAAA!
LORD IL PALAZZO!
THIS LOOKS AWFULLY FAMILIAR!
LIKE A FLUSH TOILET?
YES! EXACTLY!
THAT'S JUST WHAT I WAS THINKING OF!
YOU NEVER CEASE TO AMAZE, LORD IL PALAZZO!
I'VE LEARNED

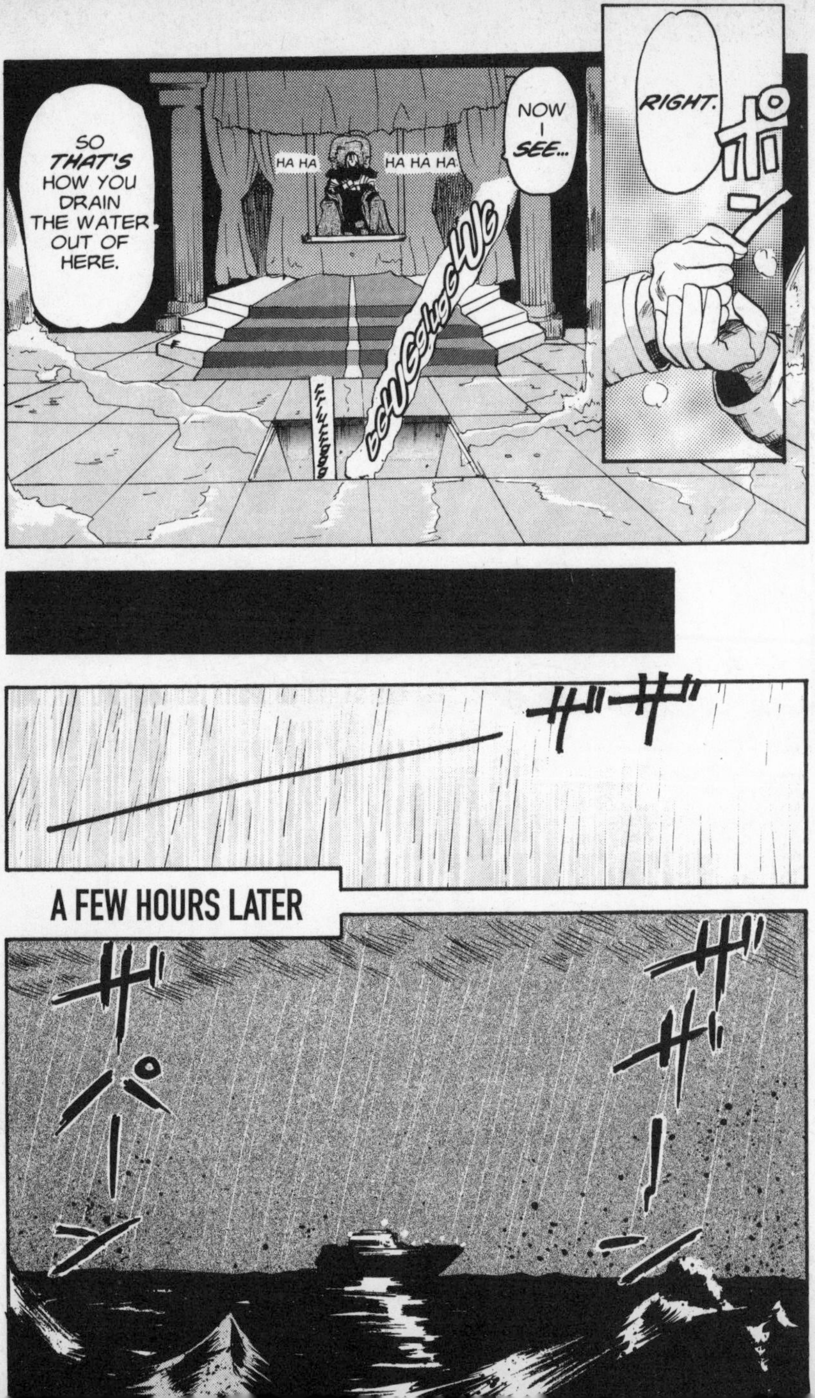

RIGHT.

NOW I SEE...

HA HA HA HA HA

SO *THAT'S* HOW YOU DRAIN THE WATER OUT OF HERE.

A FEW HOURS LATER

BOY, WE SURE LUCKED OUT-- HAVING THIS HELPFUL SHIP PASS BY US, MINCE...
I WONDER WHAT COUNTRY THEY'RE ALL FROM...?

I SURE DIDN'T KNOW THAT OUR UNDERGROUND HEADQUARTERS WAS CONNECTED TO THE OCEAN...
i might have died back there...

OH! A RADIO!

this well-developed depression

expected to pass through western Japan and into the Pacific

LOCAL STATIONS! WE MUST BE CLOSE TO SHORE!

YES!

JUST LISTEN TO THEM CHEER!
AREN'T THEY WONDERFUL PEOPLE, MINCE?
i think you have this wrong
THIS EPISODE'S SLAVES: YOKOMAEBA CHIMPATSU AND KINEMA (EVERYBODY LOVES INSECTS)

LET'S SEE... WHAT *NEWS* FROM THE WORLD TODAY....

TV 12

カチュ

...a ship carrying illegal immigrants was intercepted by the Japanese Coast Guard while approaching the coast in the pre-dawn hours of this morning...

WELL, *WELL.*

...the Immigration Bureau has begun an immediate investigation, with much concern over the international implications of...

THE GLOBE IS *YET AGAIN* IN *TURMOIL.*

IN ANY CASE, *EXCEL* SEEMS TO BE *TARDY*...
HOW *DISAPPOINTING.*

Immigration Bureau

NATIONALITY?

SECRET.

YOUR *NAME*?

I CAN REVEAL MY *CODE* NAME...

...YOUR *AGE*...?

UNSPECIFIED!

カッカッ

I MUST *COMPLIMENT* YOU UPON YOR *MASTERY* OF THE JAPANESE LANGUAGE...

END MISSION 2

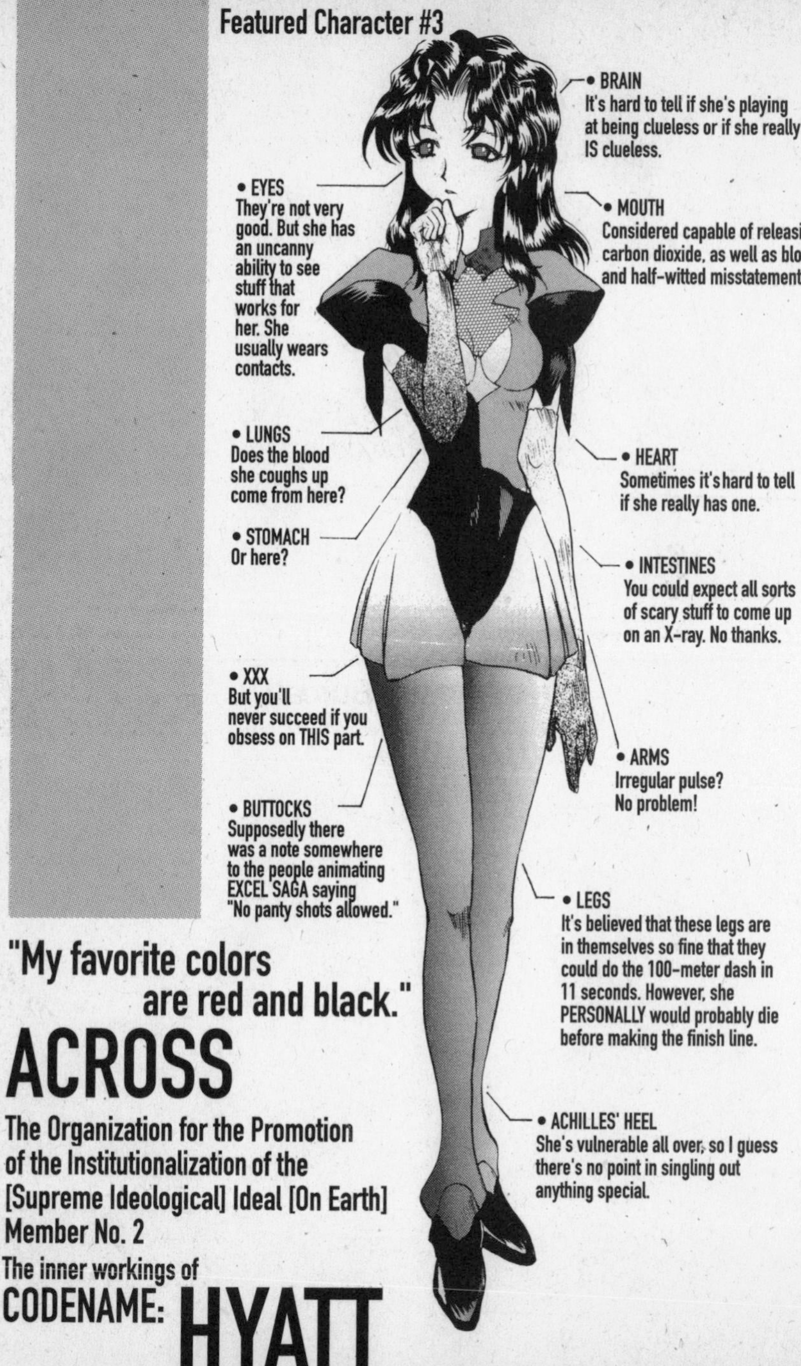
Featured Character #3
• BRAIN
It's hard to tell if she's playing at being clueless or if she really IS clueless.
• EYES
They're not very good. But she has an uncanny ability to see stuff that works for her. She usually wears contacts.
• MOUTH
Considered capable of releasing carbon dioxide, as well as blood and half-witted misstatements.
• LUNGS
Does the blood she coughs up come from here?
• HEART
Sometimes it's hard to tell if she really has one.
• STOMACH
Or here?
• INTESTINES
You could expect all sorts of scary stuff to come up on an X-ray. No thanks.
• XXX
But you'll never succeed if you obsess on THIS part.
• ARMS
Irregular pulse? No problem!
• BUTTOCKS
Supposedly there was a note somewhere to the people animating EXCEL SAGA saying "No panty shots allowed."
• LEGS
It's believed that these legs are in themselves so fine that they could do the 100-meter dash in 11 seconds. However, she PERSONALLY would probably die before making the finish line.
"My favorite colors are red and black."
ACROSS
The Organization for the Promotion of the Institutionalization of the [Supreme Ideological] Ideal [On Earth]
Member No. 2
• ACHILLES' HEEL
She's vulnerable all over, so I guess there's no point in singling out anything special.
The inner workings of
CODENAME: HYATT

EXCEL SAGA

WHAT DO...
...THE WORDS -- "WORLD CONQUEST"... MEAN TO YOU...?
IT MEANS CONQUERING HALF THE WORLD!
INTERESTING...
TO CONQUER THE WORLD, YOU CONQUER HALF OF IT! TO CONQUER THE HALF, YOU CONQUER THE HALF THAT—
[ANSWER EDITED FOR LENGTH]
—YOU CONQUER ONE ENTIRE CITY!
VERY WELL.
YOU SHALL BE INDUCTED INTO OUR RANKS...
AS A MEMBER OF OUR ORGANIZATION FOR THE PROMOTION OF THE [SUPREME IDEOLOGICAL] IDEAL [ON EARTH]... ACROSS!

YOUR CODE NAME SHALL BE...
HYATT!
MISSION 3
TODAY AND TOMORROW FOR ENCOUNTERS

HAIL, IL...
PLKOFF

UM, HELLO. WELL, I GUESS I SHOULD EXPLAIN THE SITUATION I'M IN RIGHT NOW...
I EXERCISED MY RIGHT NOT TO SELF-INCRIMINATE AND KEPT SILENT -- ONLY TO BE THROWN INTO SOME STRANGE FACILITY...

AND, JUDGING BY THE STURDINESS OF THE IRON BARS, IT SEEMS CLEAR THAT THEY WON'T SIMPLY LET ME LEAVE...
I WENT THROUGH A LOT.
REALLY.
-- SOOOO, RIGHT NOW I'M GETTING DOWN TO EARTH, DIGGING WITH THIS SPOON THEY GAVE ME FOR MY THREE HOTS.

I WONDER WHAT'S HAPPENED TO LORD IL PALAZZO...
ポイ
ポイ
ザク
ザク
ザク
THIS IS PROBABLY TOUGH FOR HIM...

ボコッ
HEY!
YES! I MADE IT OUT!

oh...
i haven't felt the warmth of the sun for so long...
its light...
...its ultraviolet rays...
its high-frequency ionizing radiation...
UM...
gal Immigrant Detention Center
WOULD YOU MIND TELLING ME WHERE I AM...?

下僕堂
GASP!

FOR HOW LONG DID I REMAIN COLLAPSED AND UNCONSCIOUS?
THREE HOURS PLUS, I BELIEVE.

I WAS JUST STARTING TO THINK ABOUT HOW I SHOULD GET RID OF YOUR BODY...
HA HA HA
THREE HOURS...
I'VE JUST BROKEN MY OLD RECORD...
MEMORY

TELL ME, DOES THIS HAPPEN TO YOU OFTEN?
WELL, YES...
BUT SO FAR I'VE ALWAYS MANAGED TO REVIVE...

I WAS HOPING TO AVOID MY FINAL COLLAPSE AT LEAST UNTIL THE DAY I COULD SEE THIS CITY...

......
...CON...
...QUERRRED...

HYATT.
YES, LORD IL PALAZZO?

WE'LL LIMIT OURSELVES TO JUST MAKING INTRODUCTIONS TODAY.
GO AHEAD AND TAKE THE REST OF THE DAY OFF...
OHHHH... IS THAT REALLLY ALL RIGHT?
...THE RRRUUUUSHHHH...

THEN ALLOW ME TO BE RUDE ENOUGH TO TAKE ADVANTAGE OF YOUR KIND OFFER...
OH, YOU DO KNOW WHERE YOUR OWN HIDEOUT IS LOCATED...?
YESSS... I BELIEEEVE... I CAN... FIND... IT...

......
パタン

ACROSS
Application for Employment
カサッ

OH.
SHAME ON ME.
ACROSS is an equal opportunity employer

I FORGOT TO INCLUDE ANYTHING HERE ABOUT A PRE-EXISTING HEALTH CONDITION.
HA HA HA HA

ENOUGH TALK!
LET'S RUMBLE!
h'llo — excel here!
BASTARDS! THEY THINK THIS PLACE IS A PUSHOVER, DO THEY...?
FIRE AT WILL!
since escaping alone seems impossible, I've been forced to instigate a prison riot!
RAISE HELL!
BURN BABY BURN!

DIVERSIONARY SQUAD!
GO FOR BROKE!

YOUR THEME SONG -- "THE CHARGE OF THE LIGHT BRIGADE!"
アアア

please understand -- i have a higher mission to accomplish!
guided by lord il palazzo, i strive to save this world!

HEYYYY! ♡

MINCE!

THERE'S ONE OVER THERE!

AACK...

MINCE?!

GOOD JOB, ROVER! GOOD BOY!

C'MON, MINCE! IT'S ME! DID YOU FORGET ALREADY?
YOU AIN'T GETTIN' AWAY!
AIM FOR THE LEGS!
AND REMEMBER, "NO EXCESSIVE FORCE", HEH HEH!
SO YOU ALREADY FORGOT THE PERSON WHO SAVED YOUR HIDE, HUH?
huh?
OH, WELL, YOU ARE ONLY A DUMB BEAST, AFTER ALL!

the end of my nightmare is near...

YES!
I CAN SEE WHAT'S OUTSIDE THE WALLS!
the free world!

now is the moment of truth!
how'd she tie me up so fast?
i knew that having had an acquaintance at work whose cousin was a pole vaulter would someday pay off!
ガ
AIEEEEEEEE!
WA-HOO!
FROM THE MUD TO THE STARS -- IN ONE SHOT!
lord il palazzoooooo!

YIKES!

WHAT THE--?

HUH?

--OH.
OKAY WOW.
boy, did i luck out...

HA HA! WELL, AREN'T YOU A CUTE ONE!

HEY, MAN! YOU'LL GET IN TROUBLE WITH THE WARDEN...!

C'MON, BOY, EAT UP! IT'LL MAKE YOU BIG AND STRONG!

PLAYIN' WITH THAT DOG AGAIN, EH? THAT'S IT -- YOU'VE GOT OVERTIME, MISTER!..

--AND I EXPECT YOU TO USE EVERY MINUTE OF IT TO BUILD THIS LITTLE GUY A PROPER DOGHOUSE!

Y-YES, WARDEN!

MINCE...
AW... POOR PUPPY...

THEY WERE REALLY ***ROUGH*** ON YOU IN THERE, ***WEREN'T*** THEY?

LET'S GO ***HOME...***
...TOGETHER.

HUH?

WHAT THE ...!?

WHAT ARE YOU DOING OUT HERE... HEY!
ARE YOU ALL RIGHT? HELLO!?

uhhhhh ....

i saw a bed of flowers... on the other side of the river ....

OH, NOTHING. ...I'M A LITTLE ANEMIC. I'M TERRIBLY SORRY TO BE A BOTHER, BUT WOULD YOU LEND ME A HAND?
YEAH... SURE.

YOU'RE FAR TOO KIND.
D... DON'T WORRY ABOUT IT...
カーン
カン
カン

SO... WHICH IS *YOUR* PLACE?
YES... *APARTMENT 204...*
カーン
カーン

YOU?! YOU'RE THE ONE THAT LIVES THERE?!
YES...
FROM *TODAY* ON...

FROM.. *TODAY* ON?
YES... I WAS TOLD TO RETIRE TO THIS *HIDEOU--* I MEAN, *COMPANY HOUSING.*

HUH. AND WHAT ABOUT THE PERSON THAT *USED* TO LIVE THERE?
I CAN'T SAY... ...I WASN'T TOLD OF ANY... *PREVIOUS* OCCUPANT...

THEN WHAT ABOUT...

...ALL THE STUFF THAT HAPPENED *BEFORE?*

PHEW.
KINDA EXHAUSTING, ISN'T IT, MINCE...?
PRISON GRAYS

HEY...

C'MON C'MON!
TAXI!!

IN THIS MEAN EXISTENCE OF OURS...
J-JUST IGNORED ME... SOB
...KINDNESS IS SURE HARD TO FIND.
...got your license plate number, you big jerk...

QUITE A PREDICAMENT, IT SEEMS...
HA HA HA...
...but i won't give up!
even if i have to fight against this entire world...
...i will remain your slave, lord il palazzo!

AH!

A SHINTO SHRINE!
LET'S REST HERE, MINCE!

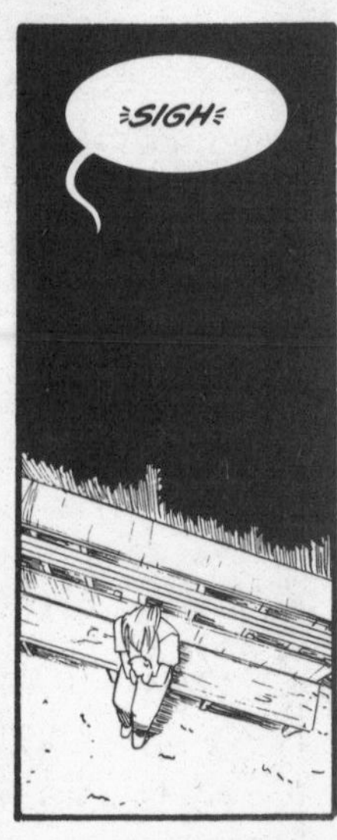
SIGH

I SURE AM HUNGRY...

HEH! DON'T WORRY!
...I'M NOT GONNA EAT YOU FOR DINNER!

...YOU'RE STRICTLY RESERVED FOR EMERGENCY RATIONS ONLY...

ブルル

ピクッ

WHAT *IS* IT, MINCE?

IS SOMETHING *THERE...?*
ザク
ザク

OH! THEY HAVE A *HORSE* AT THIS SHRINE!
MINCE! THIS HORSE IS CALLED *GOSHINME!* IT'S THE HORSE THAT THE *GODS* RIDE ON!
GO-SHINME
神馬

ブフルン
...THAT THE GODS-- *RIDE...*

OUR HORSE!
OUR GOSHINME!
GRRR! SO YOU THINK THE SHINTO RELIGION IS A PUSHOVER, HUH?
SHOOT, MEN! FILL THAT THIEVING BRAT FULL OF HOT TWIGS!
the steed of the gods! in other words, this steed belongs to lord il palazzo!
please! allow me to borrow your divine steed for a moment, my lord!

lord il palazzo!
カパラッ
カパラン
excel will be at your side in no time!
AHH...
LOOKS LIKE I'LL LIVE TO SEE ANOTHER SUNRISE AFTER ALL...
WOW, WHAT A BUZZ...
シャラ..
コクン

経南無妙法蓮華経南無妙法蓮華経南無妙法蓮

am-Myo-Ho-Ren-Ge-Kyo • Nam-Myo-

NAM MYO HO REN GE KYO
......

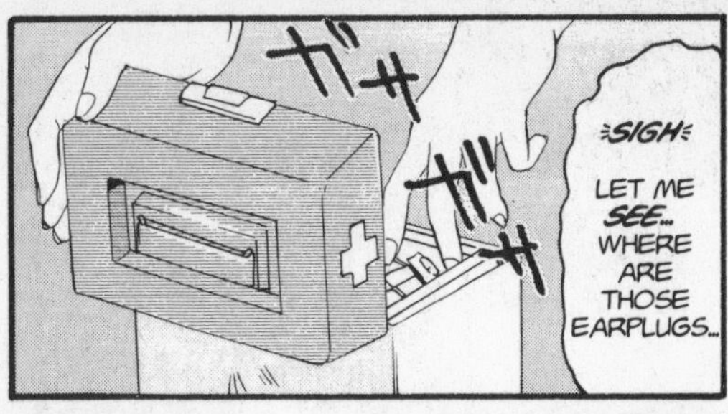
SIGH
LET ME SEE... WHERE ARE THOSE EARPLUGS...

STORY OF MY LIFE...
I JUST MOVED IN TODAY, AND ALREADY MY SLEEP IS BEING HINDERED -- AND BY A DEVOUT NICHIREN BUDDHIST CHANTING THE LOTUS SUTRA.

AH, WELL...

AHHHHHHHHH!
WHAT A GREAT DAY!
ALL RIGHT! TIME FOR THE MORNING CHUG!
MILK
HUH ?
MILK
MILK

HUH? WHAT THE--?
BASTARD! GIMME BACK MY MILK!
WHAT THE HELL ARE YOU TALKING ABOUT?
SHUT YOUR HALF & HALF HOGGIN' HOLE! AFTER YOUR THIEVIN' FEET LEFT A TRAIL LIKE THAT!
FEET? TRAIL?
YOU SHOULD ALWAYS CHEW YOUR MILK...
MUNCH CRUNCH BEFORE SWALLOWING...

GOOD MORNING, HYATT.
GOOD MORNING, LORD IL PALAZZO.
DID YOU SLEEP WELL?
YES, VERY WELL... I FEEL THAT MY GRIEVANCES HAVE ALL BEEN ALLAYED.
WELL, THAT'S GOOD TO HEAR...
HA HA HA
GOOOD MORRRRNING, SIR!

SIR! AS OF NOW --RIGHT NOW-- EXCEL IS BACK AND REPORTING FOR DUTY SIR!

ゼ ゼ

パラン

WELL. *EXCEL.*

GOOD MORNING.

YOU'RE *LATE.*
AUGH!
I HAVE A *LENGTHY* AND *DETAILED REPORT* PREPARED TO ACCOUNT FOR --!

AIEE! AIEE!

SIR, WHO MIGHT *SHE* BE?

AH, *YES.* HER NAME IS *EXCEL.*

SHE WENT *MISSING* FOR A WHILE, BUT SHE IS *ALSO* A MEMBER OF ACROSS.

I *SEE.*

NO... ENERGY... LEFT...

スッ

ゼ ゼ

YES?

I HAD NO IDEA THAT I HAD A SENIOR.
I HUMBLY OFFER MYSELF TO YOU...

OH... UH.. YEAH!
SAME HERE!

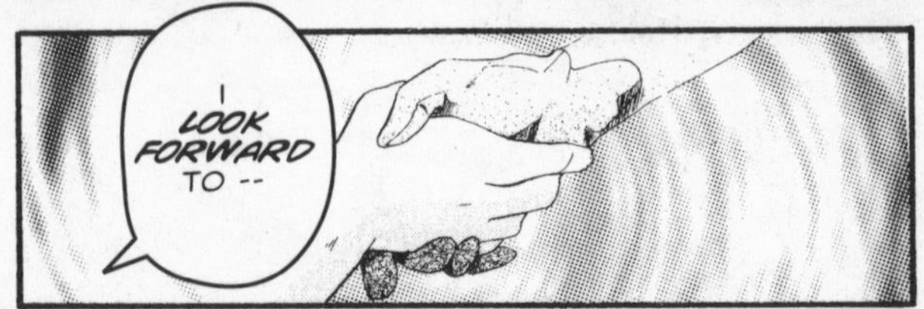

I LOOK FORWARD TO --

AAARRGGHH!

WELL, I'M DEFINITELY BACK...

IT SOUNDS LIKE YOU TWO ARE HAVING FUN..

WHAT THE--?

AAAAHHHHHHH!

BLOOD! LORD IL PALAZZO! I'M SCARED! SHE'S VOMITING BLOOD!

THE BLOOD! THE BLOOD!

END MISSION 3

NOW THEN, WHILE NOTING HOW OUR REBORN ACROSS HAS GONE THROUGH DRAMATIC EXPANSION WITH THE INFLUX OF NEW PERSONNEL...
I WILL NOW MAKE SOME ANNOUNCEMENTS REGARDING NEW ASSIGNMENT POSTINGS...
カサッ
FIRST OF ALL: FOR EXECUTIVE AND STAFF OFFICER...
...HYATT!
FOR COMBATANT...
MINCE!
AND, FINALLY...

MISSION 4
EVERYDAY LIVING PERMISSIBLE

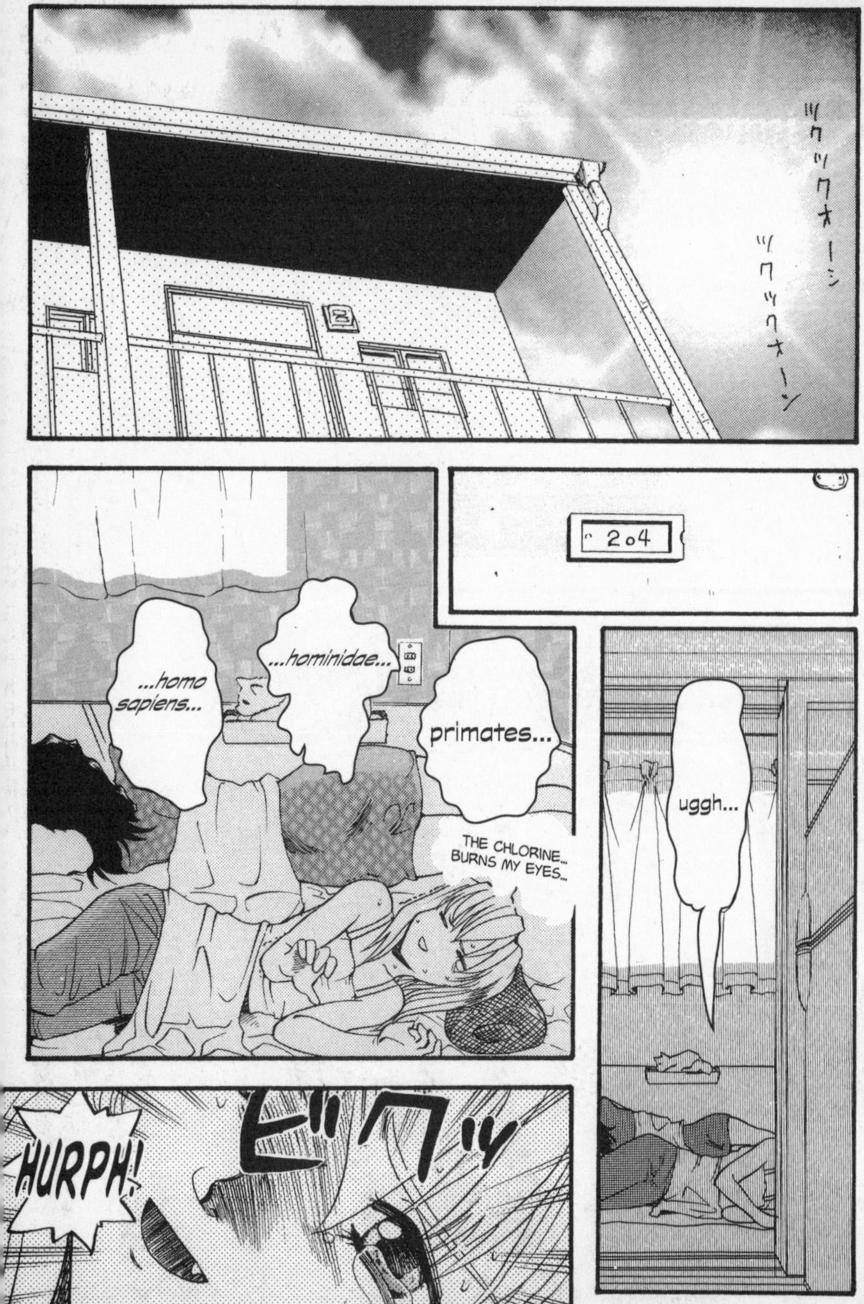

ツクツクオーーシ
ツクツクオーーシ

204
primates...
...hominidae...
...homo sapiens...
THE CHLORINE... BURNS MY EYES...

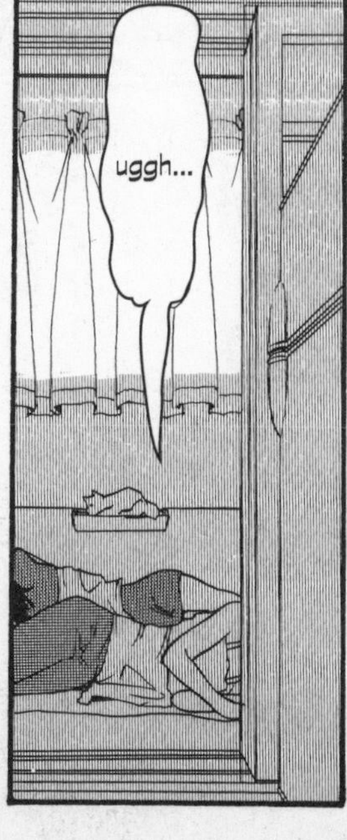
uggh...

ビクッ
HURPH!

I WONDER...
I FELT... I WAS ENJOYING A *DREAM*...
...THAT WENT *ONE STEP BEYOND* THAT WHICH THEY SAY HUMANS *SHOULD* TAKE PLEASURE IN...

SO *HOT*...
BOY! I'M AMAZED THAT YOU CAN *SLEEP* THROUGH ALL THIS HEAT, *HA-CHAN!*

THIS LOOKS REALLY BAAAAD!

THERE... ♬

WOWWWWWW! ♬

it really was hot last night!

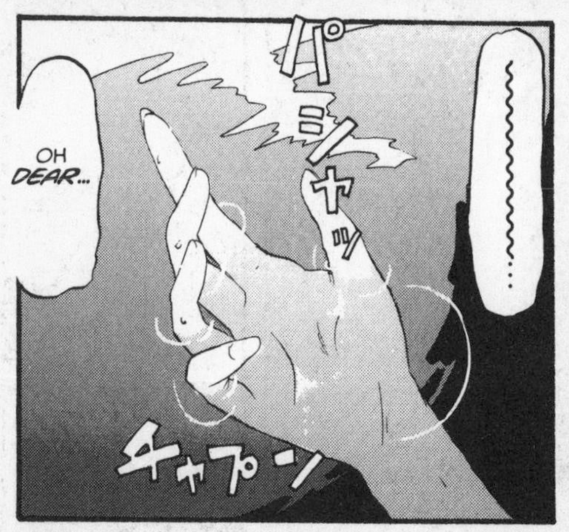
......
OH DEAR...
チャプン

...A BATHTUB?
SENIOR?
SENIOR EXCEL?
HEY, SHE'S RESUSCITATED!
SO-- WHY WAS I IN A BATHTUB?
WELL, YOU KNOW... YOU WERE COVERED IN SWEAT...
BUT I WAS STILL IN MY PAJAMAS...
yeah, but it looked like your body would disintegrate if i moved it around too much...
OH, HEY. WOULD YOU MIND IF I STARTED CALLING YOU STUFF LIKE "INSTANT POTATOES" OR "MS. SEA MONKEY"?
I DON'T UNDERSTAND WHAT THIS IS ABOUT, BUT I ASK THAT YOU KINDLY ABSTAIN.
RESOLUTE!

チリーン
BUT I SURE WONDER...
...WHAT WAS THE DEAL WITH LORD IL PALAZZO YESTERDAY...?
SUDDEN THIS MAY BE. BUT KNOW THAT FOR THE NEXT 72 HOURS--
I SHALL BE AWAY FROM THE SECRET HEADQUARTERS!

I SEE...
SO... WHAT SHOULD WE BE DOING IN THE INTERIM, SIR?
HMM...
...WHY NOT CONSIDER THIS A BELATED SUMMER VACATION?
HOW WONDERFUL!
WHERE WILL YOU BE GOING, LORD IL PALAZZO, SIR?
TO A FAR DISTANT PLACE...
YES, INDEED -- TO A PLACE SLIGHTLY DISTANT...
HIS GAZE SEEMED TO LOOK BEYOND...
BUT CHEE!
72/24 = 3 days!

WHAT SHOULD WE DO, HA-CHAN?
OOPS.

......
hey, i wonder if her skin will brown if i pour this soup base on her...

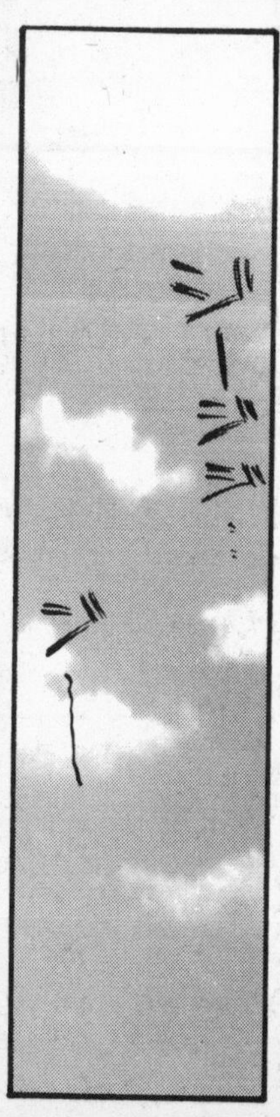

SENIOR EXCEL?
YE-E-E-S?

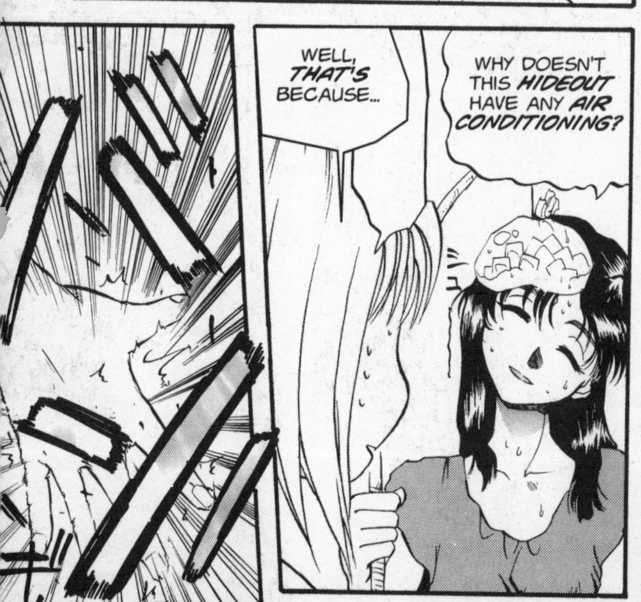
WHY DOESN'T THIS HIDEOUT HAVE ANY AIR CONDITIONING?
WELL, THAT'S BECAUSE...

しゃりーーん
カカカカ…

WHAT IS THE *SIGNIFICANCE* OF THESE *47 YEN?*
THE COMBINED *AGGREGATE* OF OUR AVAILABLE *FINANCIAL RESOURCES.*

EXCUSE ME?
OUR *TOTAL ASSETS.*

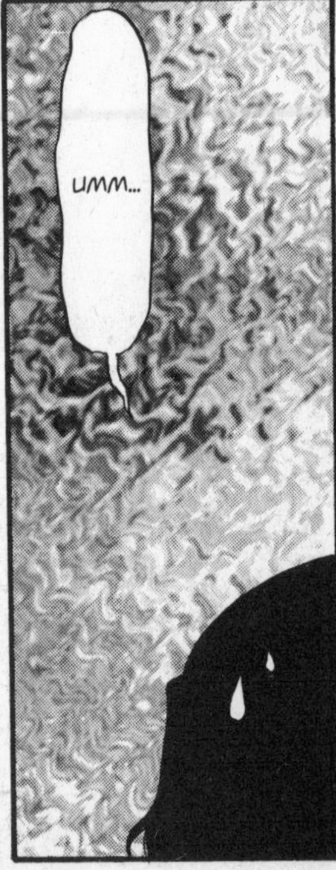
UMM...

SO HOW IS THE *CONQUEST* OF THE *CITY* BEING FINANCED?
THE *"CONQUEST" BUDGET* IS STRICTLY FOR *CONQUEST...*
LIVING EXPENSES ARE *SEPARATE.*

SO... WE MUST ENDURE FOR *TWO DAYS* WITH ONLY *THAT?*
DON'T *WORRY. REALLY...*
HA HA
ピク
IN CASE OF *CRISIS,* WE ALWAYS HAVE emergencyration *MINCE.*

わたわた
I SEE...
BUT I MUST SAY I HAVE RESERVATIONS ABOUT THIS...
ピスピス

BESIDES, I DON'T KNOW HOW TO PREPARE DOG...
YEAH. I'D IMAGINE THAT'S A MYSTERY TO MOST PEOPLE...

ピーンポーン
HELLOOOOO! ♫

I'M FROM THE NHK -- HERE TO COLLECT YOUR TELEVISION FEES...

!!

......
can't pretend we're not home...

コク

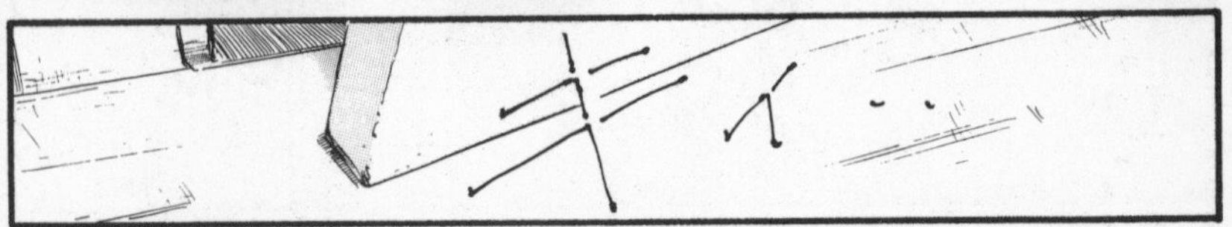
ギイ…

AHEM. AS IT IS THE DUTY OF ALL GOOD CITIZENS TO SUPPORT PUBLIC TELEVISION, AND TO ENSURE THE CONTINUED BROADCAST OF QUALITY SHOWS LIKE...

...WON'T YOU PLEASE...

C-CONTINUED... BUH-BROADCAST...
AIIEEE!
TE... LE... VISION...
FUH-FUH-FEES...
nice one!
that's the ticket, ha-chan!
EYAAAAAGGHH!

YAAAAA

HA-CHAN! THAT WAS AWESOME!
しゃわしゃわしゃわ

WHAT THE HELL'S UP WITH THIS HEATWAVE? SUMMER'S ALMOST OVER!
SO... FREAKIN'. HOT...

!?
......

WHY DO I GET THE FEELING...
...THE HEAT'S COMING FROM JUST ONE SIDE OF MY ROOM...?

I'VE HEARD ABOUT THIS SITUATION BEFORE!
HEY! C'MON!
HEY! ANYBODY IN THERE? HELLO!

HUH! EVEN THE DOOR IS ALL HOT!
WHEN YOU ENCOUNTER THIS -- THERE'S A GOOD CHANCE A FIRE IS RAGING ON THE OTHER SIDE...
CRAP! IS THIS THE REAL THING?

SOMEONE...!
HUH?

CHOKE
HOT AIR...!

... A BLAST OF --
HEY! WASSUP ?

UH... YEAH.
WE'RE IN THE MIDDLE OF AN IMPROMPTU HEAT ENDURANCE CONTEST...
LIKE, RIGHT NOW WE'RE TRYING TO BREAK OUR PREVIOUS RECORD...
A
B

I ADMIT, I THOUGHT IT WAS KIND OF A STUPID IDEA AT FIRST, BUT...
...WHOA, THAT OUTSIDE AIR'S COOL...
...ONCE YOU GET INTO IT -- YOU'RE HOOKED!

UH, HEY, WANT SOME NOODLES? A LITTLE UDON? WHADDAYA SAY?
IT'S SMOTHERED IN SEVEN-FLAVOR SPICE!

OH... YEAH?

UMPH!
OH YEAH! THEY'RE RIGHT Y'KNOW, THAT STUFF ABOUT MIND OVER MATTER!

MMFF! HFFF! WHAT THE HHFFELL ARE YOU DOING FFF?
PUTTIN' OUT THAT MOUTH BEFORE I EXTINGUISH THE REST OF YA!
ぱた ぱた
THIS APARTMENT SURE IS ROWDY...

EVERYONE'S PROB'LY JUST STRESSED OUT 'CAUSE IT'S SO HOT...
...but soon comes the season when the spirits of the dead return to their haunts. it's said they bring a chill to the air...
HERE, HA-CHAN. HAVE SOME MEDICATION.
OH... WHY THANK YOU.

......?

UM... SENIOR, THIS MEDICINE...
...WHAT MIGHT IT BE?
LE-E-ET'S SEE HERE...

UH, IT SAYS "SANTONIN"...

?
ER, SENIOR...
...COULD WE PLEASE RESERVE SUCH REMEDIES FOR DEAR MINCE HERE?
[SANTONIN = FOR ROUNDWORM]

SENIOR EXCEL, WOULD YOU LIKE SOME?
SUCH A BUZZ...
NO THANKS. THAT'S STUFF'S GOTTA BE BAD FOR MY HEALTH...

SENIOR, WHAT MIGHT YOU BE *DOING?*
JUST LOOKING AT SOME *COUPONS* HERE...
TAKE A *LOOK!* RAMEN, JUST *47 YEN!*
YES...
...AND THE *SALES TAX* IS 5%...

it's like we're under siege!
...left to starve... supplies... cut... off!
...by whom?
誰に

HEY! I WONDER IF SOMEONE WILL SEND US GIFTS FOR THE *CHŪGEN* SEASON...
NOPE. IT'S ALREADY *OVER...*
BESIDES, WE ARE IN A *SECRET* HIDEOUT...

AND, *FINALLY*, SHOULD NOT *WE* BE THE ONES TO BE SENDING GIFTS...

...TO *LORD IL PALAZZO?*

GASP! she's right!

...please come back quickly, lord il palazzo!

...and rule over the world so that honor and glory will be ours!

HONOR AND GLORY...
HAM AND GRAVY...

MI-I-IIII-I-INCE!

COULD YOU COME HERE, PLEASE?

WELL? HOW DOES SHE WEIGH IN?
HER TOTAL VOLUME?
HER FAT-TO-MUSCLE RATIO?
HER "SELL-BY-WEIGHT"?

DELIVERY, SIR.

SIGN HERE, PLEASE.
SURE.
THANK YOU, SIR.

HMMM...

PACKAGE FROM HOME, HUH...
BET IT'S SOME LEFTOVER CHŪGEN GIFTS...

WHAT AM I SUPPOSED TO DO WITH ALL THIS?
DAMMIT...
I DON'T HAVE SPACE FOR THIS CRAP...

HA-CHAAAAN...
YESSS...
LET'S MAKE SOME SOMEN NOODLES...
YOU CERTAINLY LIKE SOMEN NOODLES, SENIOR...

ピンポーン
WE AIN'T EATING IT 'CAUSE I LIKE IT. WE'RE EATING IT CAUSE IT'S ALL WE HAVE.
OOPS.
HA-CHAN...
...COULD YOU TAKE CARE OF IT?
CERTAINLY...
IF THAT'S A BILL COLLECTOR, GO COUGH UP SOME MORE BLOOD...
YES, WHO IS IT?
チャッ
OH.
YOU'RE...
HEY. HOW ARE YOU?
OH, DEAR. I CAN'T THANK YOU ENOUGH FOR YOUR PREVIOUS ASSISTANCE.
HEY, NO PROB. JUST HELPIN' OUT LIKE ANYONE ELSE WOULD.
...WHATEVER.
UM, MY FOLKS BACK HOME SENT THIS TO ME, AND I DON'T KNOW WHAT TO DO WITH IT. IF YOU WANT...

OH DEAR, OH DEAR!

MY GOODNESS! ARE YOU SURE YOU DON'T MIND?

UM, YEAH. IT'S NOTHING SPECIAL, BUT Y'KNOW...

OH! I'M DELIGHTED!

THANK YOU VERY MUCH! THIS WILL BE A REAL HELP TO US! THANK YOU!

YEAH, SURE. GLAD YOU LIKE IT...

THEN I'LL BE OFF.

Helping out on this episode: Gouchin-maru and Jinnojyou. Good luck on each of your jobs!

IS IT... HAM?

CANNED GOODS?

好運!

WHAT LUCK!

HEY, MINCE, YOU LUCKED OUT!

HELL WITH IT! EVEN CANDY WILL WORK!

I'LL *OPEN* IT AND SEE...

MAN, TO THINK SHE'D BE SO *HAPPY* OVER SOMETHING LIKE *THAT*...

MAYBE SHE'S HAVING A *TOUGH TIME* RIGHT NOW...

......

ONE... TWO...

HEH. I'M GLAD I *DID* THAT...

SOAP?

...THE GREAT WILL OF THE MACROCOSM IS TELLING US "USE THIS TO WASH IT... CLEAN IT... AND EAT IT"...

PERHAPS...
IT SAYS "MILK" ON THE LABEL, BUT WE CAN'T EAT THESE...
BLIND AS A BAT

OH, SENIOR -- IF I'M NOT MISTAKEN, THOSE ARE THE INSTRUCTIONS FOR SKINNING KITTY CATS...

LET ME SEE... FIRST YOU INJECT AIR INTO IT, RIGHT?

TOFU! FRESH TOFU FOR SALE...

END MISSION 4

A LONG JOURNEY CAN ONLY BEGIN WITH THE FIRST STEP!
IN ORDER TO CREATE THE ONE, TRUE, UNITED HUMANITY, ONE THAT LIVES UP TO THE HIGHEST IDEALS, WE MUST CONQUER THE WORLD...! ≶GASP≶...
-- BUT TO DO THAT, WE MUST BEGIN WITH CONQUERING THIS CITY, AND TO THAT END...!
...WE POSSESS A SECRET HEADQUARTERS -- ONE BEFITTING OUR "NO COMPROMISE" ATTITUDE AND DISCRIMINATING TASTE...
MAKE HASTE -- TO ACROSS HQ!
ONCE AGAIN, WE ARRIVE SECRETLY USING OUR SECRET PATH!
SENIOR-- COBWEBS ON YOUR HEAD...

MISSION 5
THOSE THAT BURN, THOSE THAT GET BURNED

SENIOR EXCEL?
YE-E-S-S?

YOU SEEM TO BE EXCEPTIONALLY WIRED UP TODAY.
YEAH!
CAN YOU TELL?

I DON'T KNOW HOW TO PUT IT, BUT WE HAVE MORE PEOPLE... IT SEEMS LIKE THE WHOLE GROUP IS COMING TOGETHER...
HUP!
I'M ALL WORKED UP WITH AMBITION FOR CONQUEST!
I SEE...

WORLD CONQUEST!
WHAT A GRAND AND IMMENSE PLAN, WON'T YOU PLEASE SAY!
OH!

"TIME IS MONEY"! I'M THINKING ABOUT SUGGESTING TO LORD IL PALAZZO THAT WE SPEED UP OUR AGENDA...
SENIOR--

...AND WON'T *YOU* PLEASE EXPLAIN THE PART YOUR *ABSENCES*... YOUR *SOI-DISANT* *"TEMP JOBS"*... PLAY IN THIS *GRAND* AND *IMMENSE* *PLAN?*

HAIL, IL PALAZZO.

AUGH!

AND THEN TO SAY "TIME IS MONEY"...
THAT STATEMENT EQUATES THE VALUE OF TIME WITH MERE CURRENCY...
YES, SIR! YES!
BUT THE PART ABOUT THE ABSENCES, SIR! IT WAS AN ACT-OF-GOD TYPE OF THINGIE!

...TO IMAGINE THAT A VALUE SYSTEM SO VULGAR EXISTS...
YOU'RE ABSOLUTELY RIGHT, SIR...
HAIIIL. IL PA LAZ-ZOOO.

NOW, THEN...
...MOVING ON TO EXCEL'S FAVORITE, THE OPERATION PLANS FOR TODAY...
HUH ?
OH! YESSIR! RIGHT, SIR!

AS PERTAINS TO THE ISSUE OF CITY CONQUEST, WE MUST PERFORCE CONSIDER THE FUTURE OF THE CITY.
UPON THIS PARTICULAR I HAVE A QUESTION TO ASK OF BOTH OF YOU...

HOW DO YOU FEEL ABOUT THE ISSUES RELATED TO WASTE MANAGEMENT ?
YES SIR!
I PUT IT OUT ON MONDAYS AND THURSDAYS !
OOPS

CRICKETS!
HORRID, HORRID CAVE CRICKETS-- EVERYWHERE!
YES. AND YOU, HYATT?
WELL...
I BELIEVE IT IS AN UNAVOIDABLE ISSUE THAT HUMANITY CANNOT CONTINUE TO IGNORE.

INDEED. HUMANITY HAS ARMED ITSELF WITH TOOLS WITH WHICH TO DEFY ITS EVOLVED BIOLOGICAL SYSTEM.
PHYLUM ARTHROPODAAA!
ORDER ORTHOPTERAAAA!
AIEEE!
ALONG WITH THEIR TECHNOLOGY, GARBAGE IS A ISSUE THAT EXCEEDS THE CAPACITY OF PEOPLE TO ADEQUATELY ADDRESS.

THEN WHAT SHALL WE DO SPECIFICALLY?
AH. THERE LIES THE QUESTION.

WHAT IS THE PREREQUISITE TO THE SOLUTION OF THIS PROBLEM? FIRST OF ALL... WE MUST HAVE AN ACCURATE GRASP OF THE PROBLEM!
YES SIR!
EAT THIS!

SIR, I TAKE IT THAT YOU ARE ORDERING US TO INVESTIGATE?
HM. YOU CATCH ON RATHER QUICKLY, HYATT.
QUITE CORRECT.
COMMENCE TO EXECUTE THE MISSION.
I HAVE HIGH HOPES FOR WHAT YOU WILL ACCOMPLISH!
RO...
ゼハゼハ
BY YOUR COM-MAND.
ROGER THAT, SIR!

204
フン
フン
キッ
ギッ
ギュッ
ギュッ
キュッ
キュッ
ギュッ
キュッ

ズリ
ズリ
ズリ
パラッ
ギュッ

Bitch...
SO... (hyatt) HA-CHAN...
YES?
DO YOU THINK MINCE IS LONELY ALL BY HERSELF?
PERHAPS WE SHOULD HAVE HAD HER ACCOMPANY US?
WOULD THAT HAVE PRESENTED ANY PROBLEMS?
I'M JUST FLASHING BACK TO THE NASTY DREAMS I'VE BEEN HAVING OF LATE...

SO, YEAH. UH, HA-CHAN(hyatt), WHAT ARE WE SUPPOSED TO DO IN TODAY'S OPERATION?
UM... WELL... I'M NOT SO SURE...

.........?
YES. YOU SEE, I'M STILL A COMPLETE NOVICE... HAVEN'T A CLUE AS TO HOW THINGS ARE RUN...

...BUT I WAS UNDER THE IMPRESSION THAT SENIOR EXCEL HAD AN ACCURATE GRASP OF THE PROBLEM.
I WAS BATTLING SIX-LEGGED DEMONS AT THE TIME YOU FORMULATED THAT IMPRESSION...

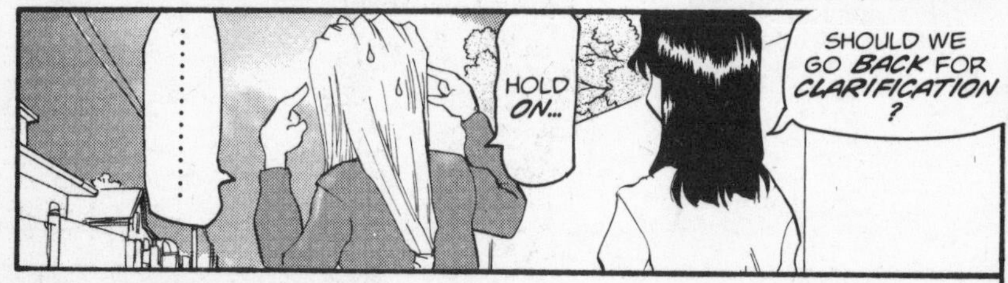
SHOULD WE GO BACK FOR CLARIFICATION?
HOLD ON...
....

SOMETHING ABOUT... GARBAGE, RIGHT?
YES! WASTE, TRASH, DEBRIS...

THEN WHY DON'T WE GO SOMEPLACE WHERE THERE IS LOTS OF GARBAGE? THAT SHOULD INSPIRE US!
IT SOUNDS LIKE A WONDERFUL IDEA!

HOW'S IT *LOOK,* SUMIYOSHI?
GUMPH...

Reet. Looks ta me this amp an' these speakaas werks fine still...
HARD TO BELIEVE THERE ARE PEOPLE WHO ARE THAT *WASTEFUL.*

Aye, an' thez people like worselves then so it aal evens oot in th' end.
GUESS YOU'RE *RIGHT.*

BUT JUST *LOOK* AT ALL THIS...

WHAT ABOUT THIS VACUUM CLEANER HERE?

JUST LOOK AT THIS CASCADE OF REFUSE, HA-CHAN (hyatt)!
YES, THIS MUST BE IT!

YOU SEE, IT'S OUR HIDEOUT NEIGHBORHOOD DAY FOR PUTTIN OUT YOUR OLD APPLIANCES...
WELL, THERE CERTAINLY SEEMS TO BE A LOT...

THEN... WHAT SHOULD WE...
JUST HOLD A SEC!

SENIOR...?

HA-CHAN (hyatt) DO YOU THINK THIS TV WORKS?

COME TO THINK OF IT, WE DON'T HAVE A TV AT OUR HIDEOUT, DO WE?
YEAH! THAT'S WHY I'M WONDERING IF WE CAN USE THIS ONE HERE...

I DON'T UNDERSTAND. THEN WHY (as i nearly expired so that he should take his leave) DID THAT NHK AGENT COME TO COLLECT OUR TELEVISION FEES?
WE LIVE IN A CHAMBER OF MYSTERY...
it's a shame you spilled your blood for his like...
血イもったいなかったね〜

IN ANY CASE, DON'T YOU THINK IT WOULD BE CONVENIENT FOR US TO HAVE A TV?
WELL, YES... I HAVE NO QUALMS, BUT...

THEN I'LL FIND SOMETHING TO HELP US CARRY IT!
UM, SENIOR...

WHAT OF THE *OPERATION*...?
てふ
てふ

Eh. This monitor'll wurk canny, seems like.

OH DEAR.
Eh? ?

ACTUALLY, THAT *TV* HAS ALREADY BEEN...
YO! ANYTHING ELSE *USABLE* AROUND *THIS* END?

I COULDN'T *FIND* MUCH...
HUH?

ACTUALLY... THAT TV'S BEEN...
How, Watanabe, this monitor is still good an' aall, I reckon.
YOU'RE...

OH! WHY, AREN'T YOU...?
WORD IS... THESE SPEAKERS AND AMPS STILL WORK...
...AND I'M GUESSING THAT VACUUM OVER THERE HAS A LITTLE LIFE LEFT IN IT...
HOWAY...

OH, DEAR. HOW KIND OF YOU. THANK YOU.
What's this, like?
SEE YA!
ズルズル

HOWAY...
JUST GET OVER HERE!
ズルズルズル
ゴロゴロ

HA-CHAAAN (hyatt) !
?
ゴロゴロ

WHAT'S WRONG?
OH, IT'S NOTHING!
I WAS SIMPLY PERPLEXED AT A DISPLAY OF THE KINDNESS OF THE MASSES!

Thez some canny salvage back there mind.
Ye knaa her, like?
SHUT UP!
NO ONE LIKES HAVING THEMSELVES SEEN AT A PLACE LIKE THAT!
Why, like? Seen so skint, yer sayin'?
CHEE! WHAT KIND OF A SAD BASTARD ARE YOU?

THERE ARE PEOPLE IN THIS WORLD WHO ARE FAR WORSE OFF THAN US!

Do ye not mean "worse off than ME" ye SADDER bastard?

HA-CHAN (hyatt), DO YOU THINK WE CAN LOAD ON ANYTHING MORE?

I BELIEVE WE CAN HANDLE A FEW MORE THINGS...
AWRIGHT, OKAY...

HEY!

A MAGNIFYING GLASS! COOOOOL!
BOY, THIS SURE TAKES ME BACK!

THESE THINGS WERE EVERYWHERE WHEN YOU WERE A KID...
SENIOR EXCEL...

WHAT?

THERE'S A COMPUTER LYING HERE. A COMPUTER!
WOW! REALLY?

YEAH! IT SAYS HERE IT'S A "TOMY TUTOR."

AND IN THIS BOX MADE OF PAULOWNIA WOOD...
IS THIS REALLY A COMPUTER?

....
MA RI KO's my real COZ

...IS A HANGING SCROLL.
MA RI KO's my real COZ
LET'S DUMP THAT.
...granted, it was already in a dump...

WELL, I SUPPOSE THAT IF WE ADDED ANYTHNG MORE, IT WOULDN'T FIT IN OUR APARTMENT.
OH DEAR.

THAT'S FINE. LET'S GET GOING HA-CHAN (hyatt)!
SENIOR EXCEL...
ONE... TWO... THREE... HUP

SENIOR...
HA-CHAN (hyatt)!

パチ
パチ
A *SUSPICIOUS FIRE!* DO YOU *THINK...?*
DELIBERATE? ARSON?

...BUT *WHEN? HOW?*
......

NOW I WANT YOU TO *REMEMBER* THIS, HA-CHAN (hyatt).
YES?

AS LONG AS WE *CONTINUE* OUR WORK, YOU AND I WILL BE THE CONSTANT TARGETS OF ATTEMPTS AT *SABOTAGE.*
SO *THIS...* IS A FORM OF *SABOTAGE?*

AND SUCH ATTEMPTS WILL BE ANSWERED...

...WITH BRUTE FORCE!

HOW'Z IT PUFF *NOW...?*
UNDER WHEEZE *CONTROL...?*
ACTUALLY, I THINK IT'S *SPREAD* SOMEWHAT...

THIS IS HOPELESS UNLESS WE GET SOME WATER OR SOMETHING!
WATER? I THOUGHT I JUST CAME *ACROSS* SOME...
...I SAW IT A *MOMENT* AGO..

THERE'S SOME *LIQUID* IN THIS...
LET'S GO!

A HEAVE AND A HO AND A--

UM, SENIOR...

I WAS WONDERING... DO YOU HAPPEN TO KNOW WHAT IS MEANT BY THIS LABEL ON THE SIDE-- THAT SAYS "HIGH OCTANE" ?
WELL...
WELL, IT MEANS THAT THIS HERE IS A VERY SPECIAL KIND OF WATER...

CHEE... YOU KNOW, I WONDERED WHY IT WENT UP LIKE THAT...

HA-CHAN... (hyatt)
WE...
...WE DID EVERYTHING WE COULD HAVE, RIGHT?
ACTUALLY, IT SEEMS WE DID EVERYTHING WE SHOULDN'T HAVE...
FALL...
...BACK!
GO!
KLANG! WOO! VOOP! HERE COMES THE FIRE TRUCK!
HEY, HA-CHAN (hyatt), YOU ARE PUSHING, RIGHT...?
OH, YES.

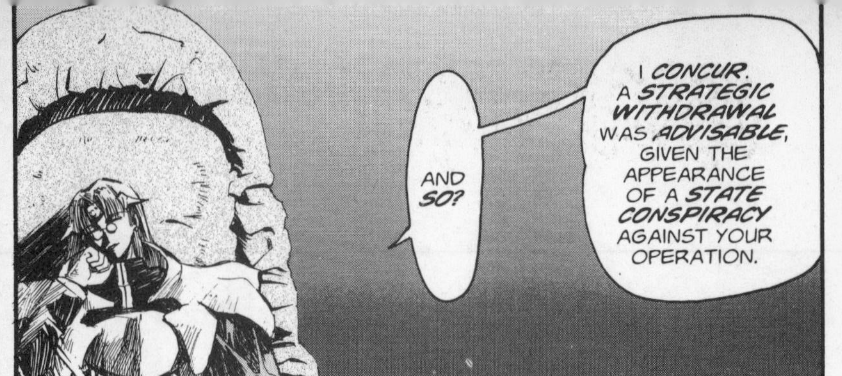

I CONCUR. A STRATEGIC WITHDRAWAL WAS ADVISABLE, GIVEN THE APPEARANCE OF A STATE CONSPIRACY AGAINST YOUR OPERATION.
AND SO?

WHAT WERE THE OBJECTIVES SECURED IN THIS OPERATION?
SIR! SIR!
WE SECURED A COLOR TV SET!

PLUS A VACUUM!
AND, UH...
...WHAT ELSE...
UM...

HEY, WHAT ELSE DID WE GET, HA-CHAAAAAAAAAAAAAAAAAAANNNN
(hyatt)
WHAT ELSE?
OH, DEAR...
...I-I'M STILL A COMPLETE NOVICE... HAVEN'T A CLUE AS TO HOW THINGS ARE RUN...

END MISSION 5

EXCEL SAGA

NOTHING'S SHOWING ON THE SCREEN...
I WONDER WHAT THIS STRANGE CONNECTOR IS FOR...
RGB MONITOR, 9-PIN INTERFACE
IT MUST HAVE BEEN BROKEN...
LET'S TOSS IT BACK.

Featured Character (?) #4

ACROSS

The Organization for the Promotion of the Institutionalization of the [Supreme Ideological] Ideal [On Earth]

ACROSS members EXCEL & HYATT's Emergency Food Source

THE TRAGEDY OF MINCE

The strange concoctions of interbreeding granted this creature a foolhardy intelligence —only enhancing the sorrow that is Mince.

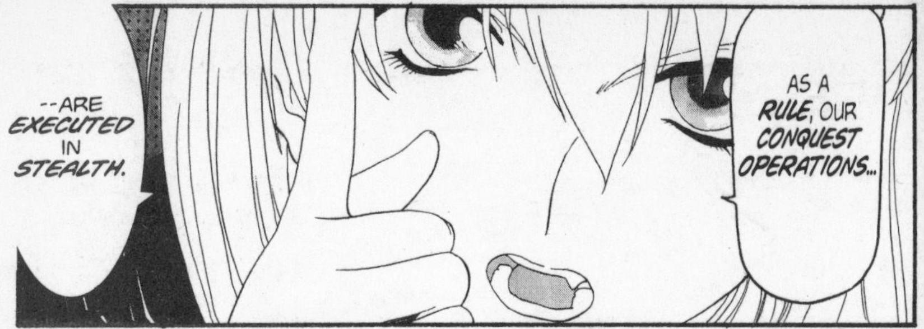
AS A RULE, OUR CONQUEST OPERATIONS...
--ARE EXECUTED IN STEALTH.

WHILE ON OPERATION, WE MUST KEEP SECRET OUR POSITION AND CONCEAL OUR IDENTITY.
IT GOES WITHOUT SAYING THAT WE CANNOT BE CAUGHT IN POSSESSION OF ANY ITEM THAT COULD IDENTIFY US IN ANY WAY.

DRIVING LICENSES, CREDIT CARDS--ALL OUT OF THE QUESTION. YES--EVEN HEALTH INSURANCE I.D.!
BUT DID YOU KNOW THAT MEDICAL BILLS ARE EXTRAORDINARILY EXPENSIVE WHEN PAID FOR OUT-OF-POCKET?
--SO, IN CONCLUSION...

HERE YOU GO...
はい
NO DOCTOR... WHEEZE
NO MEDICATION... WHEEEEZE

MISSION 6
THE UNTREATABLE UNBEKNOWNST DISEASE

OKAY, I'M OFF NOW, HA-CHAN!

YOU MAKE SURE TO GET PLENTY OF BED REST, ALL RGHT?

I MADE SOME HOT RICE GRUEL FOR YOU.
AND MAKE SURE TO CHANGE CLOTHES IF YOU SWEAT TOO MUCH.
OH... I DON'T KNOW HOW TO THANK YOU...

AND JUST IN CASE YOU NEED TO LEAVE A FAREWELL NOTE, THERE'S PAPER AND PEN IN THE BOTTOM LEFT-HAND DRAWER...
I'M SORRY FOR BEING SUCH A BURDEN... -?

SENIOR...
...WHAT DO YOU MEAN BY "JUST IN CASE"...?
SEE YOU LATER!

I SEE...
POOR HYATT.
NOW I UNDERSTAND.

THAT CERTAINLY IS A CALAMITY.
OH YEAH.
WHAT I DON'T UNDERSTAND IS HOW SHE CAN HAVE SO MUCH MEDICATION AROUND, BUT NOTHING FOR THE COMMON COLD.
COUGHS UP BLOOD FOR SOME REASON...

WELL--
WE'LL HAVE TO GET A REPLACEMENT THEN, AND QUICKLY...
LORD IL PALAZZO... LORD IL PALAZZO...

DIDN'T LAST LONG, YOU'LL AGREE!
HA HA HA
NOT YET... ...LORD IL PALAZZO.

. . .
WHAT DO YOU MEAN BY "NOT YET"?
WHAT DO YOU MEAN BY "DIDN'T LAST LONG", SIR?

REFRAIN FROM MAKING UNCLEAR STATEMENTS WITHIN HEADQUARTERS.
AIEE?!

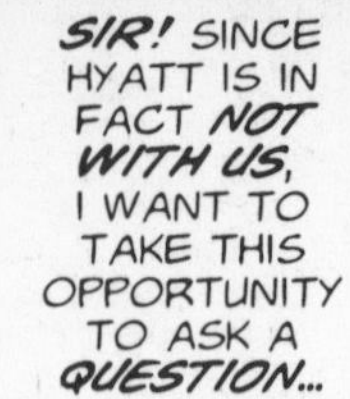
SIR! SINCE HYATT IS IN FACT NOT WITH US, I WANT TO TAKE THIS OPPORTUNITY TO ASK A QUESTION...

YES? WHAT IS IT?

WHAT IS THE QUESTION?
I UNDERSTAND WHY I AM MADE TO FALL THROUGH THE TRAP DOOR, BUT WHY HASN'T HA-CHAN BEEN DROPPED EVEN ONCE, SIR?

WELL, EXCEL -- IN THE ABSENCE OF HYATT YOU SHALL SIMPLY HAVE TO REDOUBLE YOUR OWN EFFORTS...
SIR?!
LORD IL PALAZZO?
EXCUSE ME, SIR?

WHO INDEED WOULD WISH TO LIE AWAKE AT NIGHT, OVERWHELMED WITH GUILT THAT THE UNIMAGINABLE HAD HAPPENED?
MAY I ASK ANOTHER QUESTION THEN SIR...?

......
WELL... THE ANSWER TO THAT QUESTION IS VERY SIMPLE...

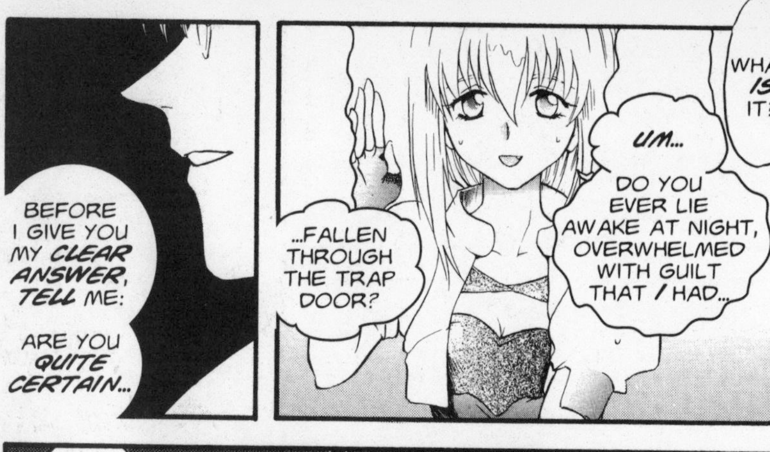
WHAT IS IT?
UM...
DO YOU EVER LIE AWAKE AT NIGHT, OVERWHELMED WITH GUILT THAT I HAD...
...FALLEN THROUGH THE TRAP DOOR?
BEFORE I GIVE YOU MY CLEAR ANSWER, TELL ME:
ARE YOU QUITE CERTAIN...

...THAT YOU WISH TO HEAR?
UM...
SIR, PLEASE LET ME THINK ABOUT THAT ONE.

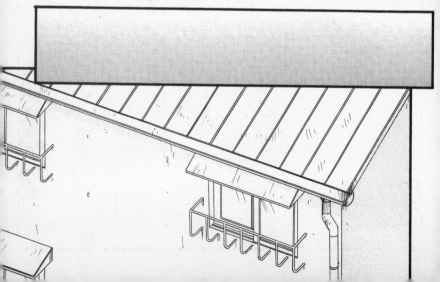

ゼィ
ハー
ハッ
ハー
ケホ
ケホ
ハッ
トテ
トテ
GAP
OPEN
PUSH→
DOOR

Right now, I could...
MISS...
MINCE
MISS...
MINCE
...

NUTRITION...

MEAT...

Ye wanna get fresh air every sae aafton ye knaa.
OH YEAH...
THANKS...

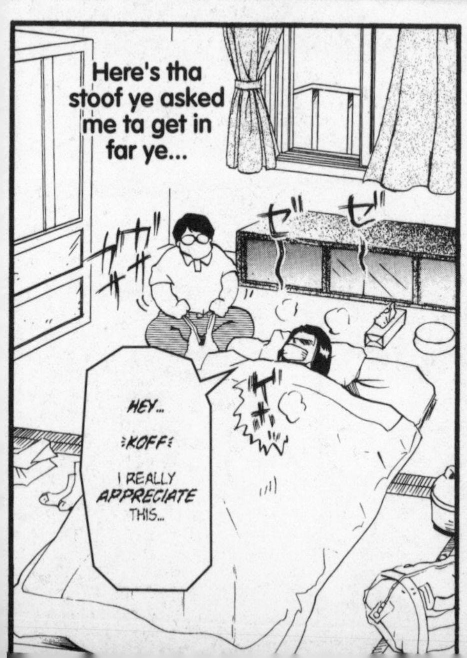

Here's tha stoof ye asked me ta get in far ye...
HEY...
⸗KOFF⸗
I REALLY APPRECIATE THIS...

Can o' peaches...

Banana...

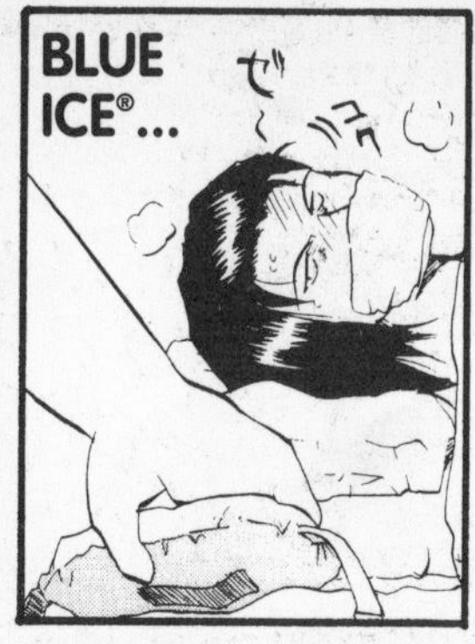
BLUE ICE®...

Aye. Wot?
WHAT ABOUT THE COLD MEDICINE I ASKED FOR?

Ye tek care o' yeself, noo...
HOLD IT!

Where I com froom thes es coold medicen, like.
I AIN'T INTERESTED IN ANY QUAINT HOMETOWN REMEDIES!

Wull why ded ye nae say so, man?
ガラ
I'M COUNTING ON YOU, ALL RIGHT?

バタン
MAN...
HAVING A COLD SUCKS.

BUT IT SURE IS NICE TO HAVE SOMEONE AROUND...
PHEW
SOMEONE YOU CAN RELY ON WHEN YOU'RE IN A JAM.

ブチャル
WHOA! THAT WAS FAST!
HEY, THANKS AGAI--

Raw eggs...
...an' saké.
YOU...!
BASTARD...

...not only did you allow me to leave early to nurse ha-chan back to health...
...you even disbursed special medical financial aid!..
...you are number one, lord il palazzo!
i can't thank you enough for your compassion, sir!
...may i be bold enough to hope that you would do the same for me!
HA HA HA
I'D RATHER NOT HAVE HYATT DIE ON US JUST LIKE THAT..

SEKI PHARMAC
...and before i know it, here's just what i need!

i guess i should start by getting some basic over-the-counter cold meds...
...and then get her something nourishing to--

--huh?

BLUE SKY...

WHITE CLOUDS...

ACK!
this is no time for me to lapse into momentary escapism!

calm down and think, excel-- THINK!
try to think of some situation where you might have dropped the money!

let's see... i twirled twice about the tobacconist at Second...
...after having the flashback, i spun thrice more for joy upon the pedestrian bridge...
...three-and-a-half somersaults i undertook on solid ground from a snap roll outside the fishmonger...
oh yes! the triangular kick-jump when that car almost ran me down on Fourth!...

DEAR GOD IN HEAVEN! the POSSIBILITIES are nearly ENDLESS!
AIEEEEEEE

i should have acknowledged that searching about randomly...
...was a tactic particularly unlikely to secure results.
uh-oh--
トボ
トボ
坂本
--oops.
... a police box.
てふ てふ
i think i'm gonna... avoid it.
くる
assistants : Gachinmaru & Kinema
Aye.
...lost and found?

HELLO! HI! HOW ARE YA!
I'M THE ONE THAT DROPPED IT!

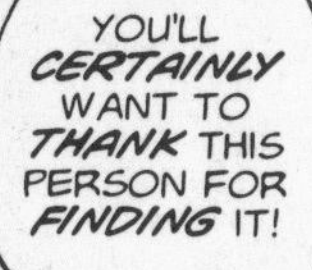
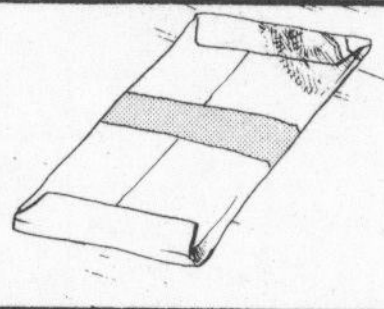
WELL! HOW LUCKY FOR YOU!
YOU'LL CERTAINLY WANT TO THANK THIS PERSON FOR FINDING IT!

THESE DAYS, FEW PEOPLE WOULD BOTHER TO TURN IN SOMETHING LIKE THIS...
Nae bather...
THANK YOU VERY MUCH! THANK YOU VERY MUCH!

NOW. SINCE THIS WILL BE A TRANSACTION INVOLVING LOST PROPERTY...
Y-E-E-S?

...WE'LL NEED TO SEE SOME SORT OF IDENTIFICATION. WOULD YOU HAPPEN TO HAVE ANY WITH Y-

...?
HUH?

I'M HO-OME...
AW, YOU'RE BOTH ASLEEP...
EXHAUSTED AFTER MANY ATTEMPTS TO BREAK FREE
OH... MINCE...
...I WAS THWARTED BY STATE AUTHORITY TODAY...
I'M HOME, HA-CHAN.. ♪
...YOU STILL ALIVE?
just a joke.

YOUR HEART...

IT'S NOT MOVING.

HA-CHAN?

MINCE...
ピス
ピス

...ANY *IDEAS* ON WHERE I CAN *BURY* HER?

OH, SENIOR.
むっくり
YOU'RE HOME EARLY.
YOICKS!

WHAT'S WRONG? YOU LOOK AS THOUGH YOU'D SEEN A GHOST...
UM... WELL... HA-CHAN...
YOUR... HEART... NO MOVEMENT...

MY... HEART?

...OH, DEAR. AGAIN?
ま
Y-YOU MAKE IT SOUND LIKE NO BIG DEAL...
...UH, HEY! YOUR COLD'S ALL GONE!
...i bet it was the virus that found its grave in there!...

noo, jest set taight...
...whilst i mek up a special hurm brew o'...
P-PLEASE... ≶WHEEZE≶
JUST LEAVE... ≶CHOKE≶

END MISSION 6

JIN-GLE BELLS ♫
JIN-GLE BELLS ♫
YEEEEEEEHAW!!!
YOU ARE ...
DID SOMETHING VERY NICE HAPPEN TO YOU, SENIOR ?
CERTAINLY MOST FESTIVE, EVEN SO EARLY IN THE MORNING TODAY ...
HUH ?
HEY... IT'S THE END OF THE YEAR.
AND ON THE SUBJECT OF A CERTAIN YEAR-END CELE-BRATION ...
TODAY IS... ♫
MERRY ... MERRY ...
OH— LORD IL PALAZ-ZO ...

CHRISTMA...

MISSION 7
A NIGHT OF NECESSARY EVIL

SECRET
ぜー
ぜー
IN THIS SEASON, ABOVE ALL OTHERS . . .
...BEING DROPPED INTO A POOL BECOMES A PRETTY HARROWING EXPERIENCE ...
YES, THE WATER MUST BE RATHER COLD, ISN'T IT?

I WONDERED WHY YOU WERE SO ELATED AND FROLICSOME ...
HOW PERFECTLY CONTEMPTIBLE.
PUNISHMENT

WHAT IS THE MEANING... BEHIND ALLOWING YOURSELF TO BE SWEPT UP IN BLIND EUPHORIA, TRIGGERED BY THE DECADENT CAPITALIST FESTIVITY OVERTAKING THE COMMON MASSES?
HAIL, IL PALAZZO ...
PLEASE EXCUSE MY RUDENESS, SIR!

OR ARE YOU A FOLLOWER OF THAT DUBIOUS RELIGION?
NO... WE REALLY AREN'T, SIR ...
I DOUBT IF PEOPLE THESE DAYS BOTHER TO THINK ABOUT WHY A FESTIVAL TAKES PLACE, SIR...

I CONCEDE THAT FESTIVALS ARE NOT IN OF THEMSELVES VILE...
BUT DO YOU NOT THINK THAT THE MOTIVES FOR CELEBRATION HAVE BECOME FAR TOO IMMORAL?
...it could be my fault, but...
Our Lord does seem to be rather upset today...

I SPEAK IN PARTICULAR OF THE PRACTICE OF FOLLOWING THE SALUTATION "MERRY" WITH THE NAME OF A CRIMINAL THAT...
SIR! LORD! LORD IL PALAZZO!!
STOP!
PLEASE STOP!

WHAT IS IT, EXCEL?

I JUST FELT THIS DISCUSSION WAS HEADING TOWARD A PARTICULARLY CAUSTIC FIELD...

COULD YOU TELL US ABOUT WHAT WE ARE TO DO TODAY, SIR?

CONQUEST PLANS...

......YES.

YOU SEE, I CONSIDER OUR OPERATIONS TO BE SACRED IN A WAY *DIFFERENT* FROM THAT OF ORGANIZED RELIGION...

OH... I FEEL THE ***SAME WAY,*** LORD IL PALAZZO...

THERE-FORE--!

...CONDUCTING OUR SACRED OPERATIONS UPON THE BIRTHDAY OF THE SUPREME CONFIDENCE TRICKSTER IN THE HISTORY OF MAN, WILL STRIKE A TONE THAT IS APPROPRIATELY SACRILEGIOUS AND...
LORD IL PAL-AZZO!!!
LORD IL PALAZZO!

じゃッ
しゃッ

......

EXPLAIN YOUR ABSURD BEHAVIOR OF LATE.
OH, NO ...uh
IT'S ONLY THAT... I HAVE THIS STRANGE FEELING THAT WE'VE JUST MADE ENEMIES OF A LARGE PERCENTAGE OF THE POPULATION OF THIS PLANET..

...AH, I SEE. YET, THE ONE OF WHOM I SPEAK TOWERS IN INFAMY ABOVE THAT GENOCIDAL MUSTACHIOED JACKBOOTED MIDGET OF A CORPORAL...LET ALONE THAT SUBWAY SARIN-GASSING, FACE-FRIED-CHICKEN-STUFFING, HAIRY-FACE-HEAD-AND-BODY-HAVING, WOULD-BE-MESSIAH OF LATE—WERE WE ONLY TO CONSIDER THE SCALE AND THE NATURE OF THE HEINOUS CRIMES MADE POSSIBLE BY HIS CHARISMA...
WHAT HIS OWN INTENTIONS WERE ARE QUITE BESIDE THE POINT ...

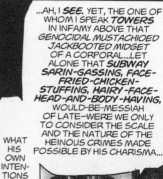

...WHY, THEN, SHOULD WE BE EAGER TO SALUTE SOMETHING LIKE THAT?
...YES, SIR!!!
ALL DOUBT IN MY HEART HAS BEEN SWEPT AWAY!

SENIOR, SENIOR ...

WHAT IS IT, *HA-CHAN* ...?
...I'M CONFUSED, AS I REALLY COULD NOT KEEP UP WITH THE CONVERSATION, SO PLEASE DON'T WORRY...

...YET SOMEHOW I AM **SURE** THAT—EVEN AS WE SPEAK—ALL THE MIDDLE EAST AND CENTRAL ASIA ARE BREAKING INTO APPLAUSE.
You know *exactly* what we're talking about, so why don't you jump in a little!

NOW, THEN! THE *MOMENT* THAT YOU HAVE BEEN *ANTICIPATING* ...

I WILL ANNOUNCE TODAY'S SCHEDULE OF OPERATIONS !!!

NOW, REGARDING TODAY'S CONQUEST PLAN #3333 ...

AH... SUCH A CHIME AS THAT I HAVE NOT HEARD IN A WHILE...
GO AHEAD... TAKE THE *CALL*, EXCEL.
Y-YES...
...YES, SIR!!!

HELLO? OH, HI.
YES, THANK YOU. WHAT? OH, RIGHT. I UNDERSTAND. I GOT IT. IT'S ALL RIGHT.
OK, EXCUSE ME, THEN!
ANOTHER PART-TIME JOB OPENING?
UM, WELL ...
TODAY BEING... YOU-KNOW-WHAT ...
PER-HAPS OUR SACRED MISSION SHOULD ...
MY *DEAR* EXCEL ...
...THIS REALLY HAS NOTHING TO DO WITH THE DATE ON THE CALENDAR, BUT...

...I'VE PREPARED A LOVELY GIFT FOR YOU.
WHAT!?
OH, MY!

MAKE SHOES, HANDBAG, A BELT... ANYTHING YOU MAY WISH.
I HAVE PROVIDED BOTH KNIFE AND MATERIALS.
CROCODILES!
FOUND THE SHANK!
JUST LIKE *TOMB RAIDER*!
hmmmmmm...

BOY, IT TAKES A LOT OF WORK TO SKIN ONE OF THE GREAT REPTILES.
AND THE UNCURED HIDE STILL SMELLS SOME-THING POWERFUL.
'mas ケーキ
GOTTA TAN THAT *PROPERLY* LATER.
SEE, IT'S LIKE THIS... YOUR CROC, HIS JAWS CAN CLAMP DOWN LIKE A SIX-INCH BENCH VISE, BUT, NOW, WHEN IT COMES TO OPENING THEM *UP* AGAIN–WELL, THAT'S A WHOLE DIFFERENT STORY.
SO, WHAT YOU WANNA DO, SEE, IS GET 'EM FROM BEHIND, PIN 'EM WITH YOUR ARMS LIKE THIS, AND THEN DRIVE THAT KNIFE IN RIGHT ABOUT HERE, STRAIGHT INTO THE SPLEEN...
YOU *LISTENIN'* TO ME, HA-CHAN?
ブル
ブル
ブル
HELLO, COULD I GET ONE OF THESE?
CER-TAINLY, THAT'LL BE 1500 YEN...
THANK YOU VERY *MUCH!*
X'm

Mommy, Mommy, it's a **rein-** deer!
THAT'S *RIGHT*, HONEY! IT'S A NICE LITTLE *REIIIIN-* DEER!

C'mon, nice little reindeer ...
Lay a lil' of that Lapland charm on 'em!

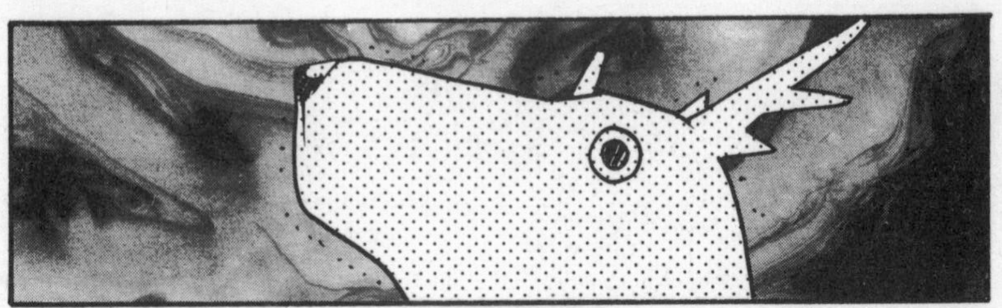

THANK YOU! COME AGAIN!
X'mas ケー

NOW, I REALIZE THAT DOING PUBLICITY PERFORMANCES AND SALES PROMOTIONS OUTSIDE IN THE COLD WINTER AIR CAN BE TOUGH ON YOU, HA-CHAN.

BUT YOU GOTTA AVOID THEM STUNTS WHAT WILL SCARE OFF ***THE PAYING CUSTOMERS.***
Uh-oh... on the verge of death...

LET'S SEE... GOT THE NOISE-MAKERS... GOT THE CHICKEN... GOT THE BOOZE...

ガチャ ガチャ

ガサ ガサッ

ONLY THING LEFT IS... THAT THING WITH-OUT...

IT AIN'T ***X-MAS.***

...YOU VERY MUCH!

OH, HELLO. CAN I HELP YOU ...

I'D LIKE ONE FIIIIINE-LOOKIN' CAKE.
COIT'-NLY!

はははは
?

HOW'Z 'BOUT A DIS-COUNT?
NO CAN DO, AMIGO!

HMM, OKAY. NO CAN DO THE HOW'Z 'BOUT A DIS-COUNT, HUH?
LEMME SEE...
......

OH. SAY, MISTER ...
HOW'Z 'BOUT THIS ?

BUY ONE... GET ONE FREE?

カキキャキーン
NEXT YOU'RE GONNA TELL ME THE PRICE FOR ONE IS 3000 YEN.
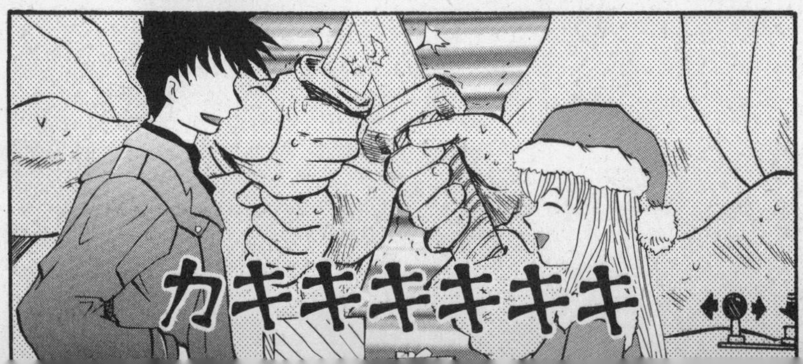
カキキキキキキ

Heh.
YOU'RE THE FIRST ONE WHO EVER...
...GOT *ME* TO PAY FULL PRICE FOR CAKE...
I GOT THIS INKLING... THAT WE'LL MEET AGAIN... *SOME-WHERE...* SOME-TIME.
BOY, THIS WORLD IS FULL OF STRANGE PEOPLE.
I'M ALL WORN OUT.
*HA-*CHAN... IF YOU'RE FEELING A LITTLE *BETTER* NOW, CAN WE TRADE PLACES, AND...
HUH?

huh?
HUH?

I LEFT YOU RIGHT HERE... didn't I?
like, here.

WHERE COULD SHE HAVE GONE IN HER CONDITI...

Could it be she's fallen victim to the recent crime wave?
Has she been... ABDUCTED?

If that's the case... HA-CHAN?!

HAS OUR COVER BEEN BLOWN?

when you're dressed like this... what difference does it make?

oh, boy. OHHHH, BOY.
HOLD ON A MINUTE; NOW, IF I'M NOT MISTAKEN, THAT'S THE DOPPLER EFFECT.
DISPATCHER DESCRIBED THE COLLAPSED INDIVIDUAL AS "CUTE, YET SCARY!"
HRK! I'VE NEVER SEEN ANYTHING LIKE IT!
WHAT THE HELL HAPPENED?
LIFT UP THE LEGS!
EASY, NOW! EASY
LET'S GO!
HURRY!!!

……

OH. BOY.

病院

カーン

DAMNIT! WHY DO WE HAVE TO GET A TRAUMA PATIENT ON A DAY LIKE *THIS?*

I'M SORRY, DOCTOR... BUT THERE WAS NO ONE ELSE ON CALL...

DO YOU HAVE *ANY* IDEA WHAT I WENT THROUGH TO SCHEDULE THE ROUNDS SO THAT I COULD BED ALL THE NEW NURSES?!

非常口

NO, DOCTOR– AND I REALLY DON'T WANT TO KNOW!

カーン

ALL RIGHT! GIVE ME A RUN-DOWN!

UM...NO ID ON THE PATIENT, BUT ...
...SHE'S A young woman ...

TO SAVE THE LIVES OF ALL WHO SEEK OUR HELP!
THAT, NURSE- IS OUR MISSION AS DOCTORS!!!
uhh . . .

HA-RUMPH!

A+
well done, nurse!
...do you really... have to stick on the gold stars, too?

BUT... YOU, THERE!
YES, DOCTOR?
I WASTOLD THIS PATIENT'S CONDITION WAS CRITICAL- WHERE'S THE RESPIRATOR... THE DEFIB-RILLATOR???

YES, WELL... THIS PA- TIENT ...

SHE HASN'T EXHIBITED ANY VITAL SIGNS...

Thanks: K. Serikawa. Gekichin Maru, Chur_sh_

YOU!
YES, DOCTOR ?

ARE YOU FREE TONIGHT ?!
EXCUSE ME? DOCTOR? DOCTOR !!

WHAT ABOUT THAT *SPEECH* YOU JUST MADE– ABOUT YOUR MISSION TO SAVE ALL LIVES!?
WHAT!?
WHEN? THAT DOESN'T EVEN SOUND LIKE ME!

LOOK. I'M NOT USUALLY ONE TO BOAST–BUT WHILE I'VE MANAGED TO LOSE MANY A LIVING PATIENT, I'VE NEVER BROUGHT A DEAD ONE *BACK* TO LIFE.
THAT'S A *BOAST*?
this could be my chance to marry into wealth...

...umm, Doctor ...

NOW WHAT!?
WELL . . .

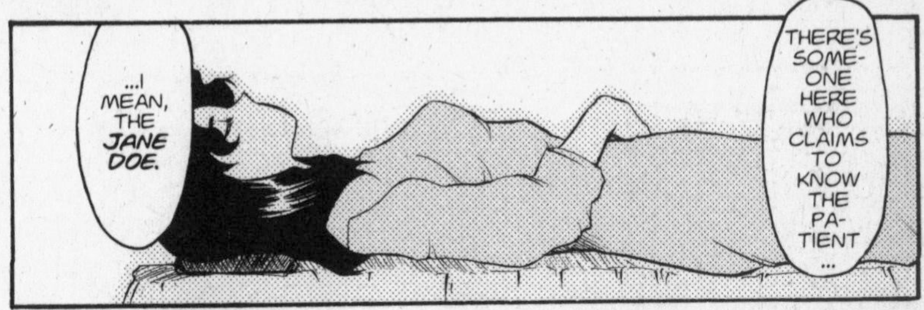
THERE'S SOME-ONE HERE WHO CLAIMS TO KNOW THE PA-TIENT ...
...I MEAN, THE JANE DOE.

ALL RIGHT, THEY CAN COME IN.
PLEASE.

HEY, THERE YOU ARE.
HA-CHAAAAAN!

WE SHARE YOUR LOSS . . .
GEEZ, HA-CHAN. I CAN'T TAKE YOU ANYWHERE.

WE DID EVERYTHING WE COULD.
WHEN?!
SHE'S STIFF AS A TWO-BY-FOUR.
OH, OKAY.
SHUT UP—I BEG OF YOU.
I UNDERSTAND.

LET'S GO HOME, HA-CHAN ...
she.. she must be in denial ...
WAKE UUUUUP!
NOW, YOU LISTEN TO ME. I'M A DOCTOR. SHE daid.

OH, SENIOR—GOOD MORNING.
COME ON. LET'S GET GOING.

THANKS FOR EVERYTHING!
OH, YES. PLEASE TAKE CARE ...

WHAT IS IT, SENIOR? WHAT'S *WRONG*?

I WARN YOU, HA-CHAN... IF YOU KEEP ON AS YOU HAVE, CHALLENGING OUR VERY UNDERSTANDING OF LIFE...

THEY **WILL** START PERFORMING ***EXPERIMENTS*** ON YOU.

CHEERS!
Not too many lasses aboot seems like.

SO? ALL GUYS IS OK, TOO!
IT'S GETTIN' TO BE RI-god-damn-DICU-LOUS!
Don't cry in your beer, man.
HEY, Y' KNOW...

I MEAN... SINCE I'M HERE, I'M NOT COMPLAIN-ING OR ANYTHING, BUT WHAT'S UP WITH THIS PARTY?
DON'T YOU HAVE ANY FRIENDS?
HEY! DON'T YOU KNOW ...

...I TRIED TO GET EVERYONE IN THE BUILDING TO COME...BUT HALF WEREN'T AROUND...AND THE OTHER HALF DIDN'T SHOW UP.
SOMEONE ACTUALLY STILL GOES FOR THAT "PLEASE WON'T YOU BE MY NEIGHBOR" CRAP?

HEY! WE ALL LIVE UNDER THE SAME ROOF—WHAT'S WRONG WITH A LITTLE SOCIAL INTER-ACTION? GETTIN' TO KNOW YOU! GETTIN' TO KNOW ALL ABOUT YOU!
AW, GIMME SOME MORE OF THAT CORN, MAN!
Thez not too many mates aboot either, mind.

HEY, I JUST REALIZED— I DON'T KNOW ANY OF YOUR NAMES!
OK, MY NAME'S IWATA. NORIKUNI IWATA! END OF INTRO!
YEAH, WHATEVER . . .

AND YOU ?
WATA-NABE. MY NAME IS WATANABE.
Stop pointing at people.
AWRIGHT!

...WHAT ABOUT THIS GUY HERE WITH THE SINGULAR AURA OR PRESENCE ???
....
HIS NAME IS SUMI-YOSHI... AND HE LIVES ON THE GROUND FLOOR.

I'm the singular Sumi-yoshi ...
Nice to meet you an' aal..
YEAH, UM... NICE TO MEET YOU, TOO...
Over-whelm-ing.

NOW THAT WE'VE FINISHED THE INTRODUCTIONS, LET ME ASK YOU SOMETHING, MY DEAR WATANABE.
HUH? WHAT ?

WHY DID YOU PICK UP TWO CAKES?
I already had one.
gak!

IN YOUR HOME TOWN, IS IT, LIKE, ONE CAKE PER PERSON?
One whole cake?
I mean, where I come from, it's just one slice.
OF COURSE NOT!

I BET YOU GOT HUSTLED BY THAT GIRL WORKING THE OUTDOOR STAND!
DAMN IT—HOW DID YOU KNOW?!?
Erm. This is too much even for mesel'.

MAN! YOU FELL FOR THAT TRICK!?
ぷわははは
SHADDAP! I GOT IT ALL PLANNED OUT... SEE?
I THOUGHT THIS ONE THROUGH...

YEAH? WHAT DID YOU HAVE IN MIND?
WELL, IT'S LIKE THIS...

I WAS THINKING...

OH, DEAR!
ARE YOU SURE ABOUT THIS?

NO... WE ENDED UP BUYING TOO MANY, SO...
DON'T WORRY ABOUT IT.
I FEEL GUILTY, RECI-EVING SO MANY GIFTS FROM YOU...

I DON'T KNOW HOW TO THANK YOU...
WELL, um, RIGHT NOW...

GO! GO!
GO!
...uh, WE GOT THIS PARTY GOING ON... EVERYONE IN THE BUILDING IS INVITED ...WOULD YOU LIKE TO COME?
Oh, HOW WONDER-FUL...

BOO
BOO
BOO
UNFOR-TUNATELY, I DON'T FEEL SO WELL...
HEY- DON'T WORRY ABOUT IT. I MEAN, IF YOU CAN'T-

BUT THANK YOU VERY MUCH FOR OFFER-ING.
BE SEEING YOU.

?
WHAT?

WATANABE! YOU DELIBERATELY CONCEALED YOUR KNOWLEDGE OF A BEAUTIFUL WOMAN LIVING NEXT TO YOU!!!
HOW'D THE TWO OF YOU GET TO BE SO friendly ALL OF A SUDDEN !?
"CONCEALED MY KNOWLEDGE" ???
Ye divven't hev t' get angry ye knaa.

SENIOR EXCEL ...
LAY OFF ME, MAN!
Strip this schemer down!
...OUR NEIGHBOR HAS GIVEN US A CAKE.

HA-CHAN ...
YOU DO REALIZE WE ALREADY GOT TO TAKE HOME ALL THE CAKES WE COULDN'T SELL...
WELL, YES.. BUT I JUST COULDN'T TURN IT DOWN ...

SAY, HA-CHAN... I WAS JUST WONDERING...
DIDN'T HE SEEM TO BE, WELL ...A LITTLE DIFFERENT, TODAY?
WHO, SENIOR ?

LORD IL PALAZZO... DIDN'T HE SEEM TO BE IN A BAD MOOD TODAY...?
OH... DID YOU THINK SO?

HE SEEMED TO ME AS IF HE WAS LOOKING AHEAD TO SOME-THING ...
I WOULD SAY HE ALMOST SEEMED ELATED.

WELL, COME TO THINK OF IT... hmm...
HEY, *MAYBE* ...

...MAYBE THERE'S A **MAJOR OPERATION** STARTING SOON— SOMETHING ON A SCALE WE CAN HARDLY IMAGINE?
OH— THAT WOULD BE *WONDER-FUL.*

END MISSION 7

Featured Characters # (Whole Lot)

...enes from the Personal Life of Rikdo Koshi Vol.①

We Who Get Wrapped Up

...and if you go into the water? Crocodiles!

Goddamnit, do some work.

We; Those Extraordinary

THE QUIET ASSIST-ANT: MR. #87.
'ello.
HE COMES EVERY TIME TO HELP OUT.

ON CERTAIN DAYS OF THE WEEK ...HE BRINGS A VIDEO TAPE.
Can you record it for me?
HE'S A SHY MAN...THAT WILL ONLY RELUCTANTLY ASK ME TO TAPE A CERTAIN TV PROGRAM.
Y-Yes...

ANO-THER NICE THING ABOUT HIM...
Any tanks to draw this time?
Oh, no you don't.
How about Saint T--!?
Of course not.
A SENSE OF TASTE.

RECENTLY, I FELT RATHER GUILTY ABOUT SOME THOUGHT-LESS REMARKS MADE BY MY NEPHEW.
MOMMY! There's a strange old man here!
I COULD THINK OF NOTHING TO SAY TO SOFTEN THE SITUATION.

exact same age

DISCLAIMER: WILL NOT ACTUALLY GO INTO SPACE

IN AUGUST! THE NEXT VOLUME OF EXCEL SAGA!

Let's go...

...TO SPACE !!!

A MYSTERIOUS ORGANIZATION APPEARS BEFORE THE PATH OF ACROSS!

...and now, two ambitions are set...

VS

FOR A FATEFUL CONVERGENCE!

DISCLAIMER: THERE WON'T BE ANY OF THIS EITHER

Look out for it! Keep your eyes open! Or at least *try* to keep them open, okay?

Let's run...

...TO OUR ***FUTURE*** !!!

Guide to *Excel Saga* 01's Sound Effects!

Most of Rikdo Koshi's original sound FX are left in their original Japanese in the Viz edition of *Excel Saga*; exceptions being handwritten dialogue and "drawn" notes that have the character of captions (for example, the graph on page 43). Sound FX are listed first with the literal Japanese reading of the sound, followed with how the sound might be "heard" as an English-language sound effect, then a description of what the sound effect represents. If there are different or multiple sound FX in the same panel, an extra number will be added to the index to show them apart. Remember all numbers are given in the original Japanese reading order: right-to-left.

Although these sounds are all listed as "FX," they are of two types: onomatopoeia (in Japanese, *giseigo*) where the writing is used in an attempt to imitate the actual sound of something happening, and mimesis (in Japanese, *gitaigo*) where the writing is used to attempt to convey rhetorically a state, mood, or condition. Whereas the first type of FX will invariably be portrayed with kana, the second may use kana and/or kanji. A good example of both types of FX in action can be seen on page 43, where the mimetic depiction of Mince's stress is alongside the onomatopoeic sound of her wheezing breath. Onomatopoeia notes: *Sound* refers to audible sounds being generated somehow. *Movement* refers to the physical movement, or lack of movement, of something; not audible or mostly not audible. *Depiction* refers to the psychological state of something or someone.

Note that at the risk of this manga appearing only 86% authentic, Mission 1 has retouched sound effects, whereas the rest of *Excel Saga* Vol. 01 is non-retouched. This is an experiment (in terror, perhaps); please contact *Oubliette* c/o Excel Saga, VIZ, LLC, P.O. Box 77064, San Francisco, CA, 94107 and let us know which way of doing it you like better. Huh-huh, I said "doing it."

Guide to *Excel Saga* 01's Sound Effects!

32-1	O/M	*zZgUSHuSHuSHuSH* (sound, water gushing in at a thunderous pace)
33-1	O/M	*vViSHiSHiSHiSH* (sound, water gushing out like a powerful shower head)
33-2	O/M	*thPlaSHpLAshPlaSHpLAsh* (sound, large flow of water, thrashing down)
33-3	O/M	*phffft* (sound, Excel blowing into decoy)
33-4	O/M	*phVLupVLupVLupVLup* (sound, water pouring down)
34-5	O/M	blush, blush (depiction,
35-3	O/M	*spLAsh* (sound, water)
35-3	O/M (black)	*zPLasssh* (sound, water)
	O/M (white)	*HUMPH* (depiction, Excel lunging out)
	O/M (black)	*zPLasssh* (sound, water)
35-5	O/M (black)	*fumpht* (sound, stamping sound)
	O/M (white)	SHOCK
36-2	O/M	*pplshh* (sound, water sound)
36-3	O/M	*dingadingadinga* (sound, alarm ring)
36-4	O/M	*dingadingadinga* (sound, alarm ring)
36-5	O/M	*chk DING!...* (sound, alarm shut off)
37-1	O/M	*swing swing* (depiction, rope end ominously swinging back and forth, like a noose)
	O/M	*thPlaSHaPlaSHaPlasha* (sound, fluttering kicking motion against water)
37-1	O/M	heh heh heh... (sound, Excel laughing but somewhat nervously)
37-2	O/M	*blub blub blub* (depiction, submerging)
	O/M	*SHHHHHHH*(sound, water gushing in at a thunderous pace)
37-3	O/M	*SHHHH SHHHHHHH* (sound, strong pouring rain)
37-4	O/M	*zzzGLuSHHGLuSHHGLuSH* (sound, huge amount of water moving about)
38-1	O/M	*thPLAsh SPLAshh* (sound, cutting through water)
38-2	O/M	*zZSHSHSHShhh* (sound, cutting through water)
38-3	O/M	*skreeech* (sound, brake sound)
	O/M	*shlooosh* (coming to stop in water)
38-4	O/M	*klunk* (sound, mail going through flap)
39-1	O/M	*shloshshloshshlosh* (depiction, large object floating by)
39-2	O/M	*plupp plupp* (depiction, the state of objects floating down the river)
39-3	O/M	yelp! *Hyap! Hyap!* (sound, cute barking)
39-6	O/M	*mm-hmm!* (sound, murmuring speech)
	O/M	FLINCH! (depiction, flinch)
40-3	O/M (above)	*yuff yuff yuff* (sound, cute dog bark)
	O/M (below)	*drip drip* (sound and depiction, water dropping)
40-4	O/M (below)	*drip drip* (sound and depiction, water dropping)
41-1	O/M	*thrPLAsh suPLAsh* (sound, cutting through water)
41-2	O/M	*zZZSHSHSHShhh* (sound, strong pouring rain)
41-3	O/M	*zzzSHSHSHShhh* (sound, strong pouring rain)
41-6	O/M	*shlosh shloshhhh* (sound, noisily being pushed away by water)
42-1	O/M	*TWINCH* (depiction, fastening something tight or closing a grip on something)
42-2	O/M	*SHWINCH* (depiction, dramatic fastening something tight or closing a grip on something)
42-3	O/M	*zZZZSHSHSHShhh* (sound, cutting through water)
42-4	O/M	(to left and right of Excel) *thrPLAsh SuPLAshhh* (sound, cutting through water)
43-1	O/M	*bTHMP* (sound, door closing)
43-3	text	*STRESS*
	O/M	*wheeze wheeze* (sound, Mince)
43-4	O/M	*rubb rubbb* (depiction, drying Mince off with towel)
43-6	O/M (above graph)	*vrrrrNNNGG!!* (depiction, line shooting up high)
43-8	O/M (white)	*kKLUNK*
	O/M (black)	*shSHING* (depiction, dramatic presentation of shiny metallic object)
	O/M	*vVRRRIPPPP!* (depiction, line shooting up high, fast)
44-1	O/M (white)	*KRASH* (sound, something breaking)
	O/M (black)	*kSHArrnkkkk* (sound, glass shattering)
	O/M (black)	*rrrRUF! RrrRUFF!* (sound, cute dog bark)
	O/M	*kTHUD* (sound, thud sound)
44-2	O/M	*klunk klunk* (sound, the metal kettle moving about)
	O/M	*kTHMPthump* (sound, thud sound)
	O/M	*kSHNK* (sound, things shattering apart as it falls down)
	O/M	BANG (sound, something hitting)
	O/M	*rrrRUFF!* (sound, cute dog bark)
	O/M	*yuff!* (sound, cute dog whine)
44-3	O/M	*kSHNK* (sound, things shattering apart as it falls down)
	O/M	*rrrRUFF!* (sound, cute dog bark)
	O/M	*kTHMP* (sound, thud sound)
	O/M	*rrrrrrRUFF!* (sound, cute dog bark)
44-4	O/M	*yuff!* (sound, cute dog whine)
	O/M	*kSHNK* (sound, things shattering apart as it falls down)
	O/M	(white, above hand) KKLUNK (depiction, object rolling about)
	O/M	(black, under hand) grrrppp (depiction, holding something tight)
44-6	O/M	*bang thud bash crash* (sound, fierce flailing about)
45-1	O/M	*kCHNK* (sound, door opening)
45-3	O/M	*kTHMP kTHMP kTHMP kTHMP* (depiction, striding strong, forceful motion)
45-4	O/M	*k-POW!* (sound and depiction, thunderous punch)
46-1	O/M	*kTHunk* (sound and depiction, a jabbing motion)
	O/M	*kRACK!* (sound and depiction, something being broken or similar)
	O/M	*THUD* (sound, heavy impact)
46-2	O/M	*pringpringpringpring* (sound, cute phone ring)
46-3	O/M	*pringpringpringpring* (sound, cute phone ring)
46-4	O/M	*peep!* (sound, electronic peep sound)
	O/M	*kTHUDTHUD* (sound, repeated hits)
	O/M	*kTHUD* (sound, impact)
	O/M	*kLUNk* (sound, something being knocked about)
	O/M	*skMAshhh* (sound, something being smashed)
	O/M	*nNNN* (depiction, sound stopping)
	O/M	*pip* (sound, electronic peep sound)
46-5	O/M	*kANg kANg kANg* (sound, metallic)
46-6	O/M	*kSHLMP* (sound and depiction, something moving after being hit)
46-7	O/M	*tunk* (sound, metallic tap)
47-1	O/M	*kANG kANG kANG* (sound, metallic)
	O/M	*zzzSHHHSHSHSHShhh* (sound, strong pouring rain)
47-3	O/M	*gng gng gng gng gng gnd* (sound and depiction, heavy doleful feeling)
47-4	O/M	*vvvmmmmmm* (sound, ambient-large not very personable hall feel)
47-5	O/M	*blublublublublbbbb* (sound, bubbling)
48-1	O/M	(black, small) *chSPLUCH* (sound, bursting out)
	O/M	(white) *shpp* (sound, water sound)
48-2	O/M	shpp (sound, water sound)
	O/M	*cough* (sound, Excel coughing)
	O/M	SHAKE SHAKE SHAKE (movement, shaking head violently)
	O/M	*spatter spatter* (depiction, water being flung off)
	O/M	*cough KAFF* (sound, Excel coughing)
48-3	O/M	*phhLUPphhLUPphhLUPphhLUP* (sound, water pouring down)
48-5	O/M	*splish* (sound, water sound)
	O/M	*splish* (sound, water sound)
49-2	O/M	GASP! (depiction and sound)
49-4	O/M	zzzZSHSHSHShhh (sound, strong pouring rain, but also water generally)
49-5	O/M	zzzZSHSHSHShhh (sound, strong pouring rain)
49-6	O/M (black)	*thrPLAsh suPLAsh* (sound, cutting through water)
	O/M (white)	*k-CLUNK* (sound, something being activated)

Guide to *Excel Saga* 01's Sound Effects!

50-1	O/M	zZZngUSHuSHuSHuSH (depiction, massive water flow)
50-2	O/M	gUSHuSHuSHuSH
50-3	O/M (white)	thtPLAsh ssPLAsh (sound, cutting through water,strong)
50-5	O/M	znnggPRRRRRSHHH (sound, massive flush)
50-6	O/M	RRRRRRR(sound, roaring sound)
51-1	O/M	fwmp (sound, stamping sound)
51-2	O/M	bGLUGglugGLUG… (sound, bubbling flush)
	O/M	rrrlurrrrgg… (sound, last gurgling sound)
51-4	O/M	zzzSHHshhSHHHHH (sound, strong pouring rain)
51-5	O/M	spLAshhh sSpLAshkk (sound, crashing waves)
52-1	O/M (black)	chuGGchuGGchuGGchuGGchuGG (sound, heavy engine)
	O/M (white)	KRRSHH KRRSHH (sound, cutting through water, strong)
57-4	O/M	zzzzSHING (depiction and movement, going into pose)
57-5	O/M	FWOOMP (depiction and movement, going into pose, extra dramatic)
59-1	O/M	SSSPLUSsshT! (sound and movement, great gout of Hyatt's coughed-up blood hitting the floor, dramatic)
60-3	O/M (white)	pfft pfft (sound and depiction, tossing light objects)
	O/M (black)	sgitch sgicth (sound, digging in small clumps)
60-4	O/M	kPLOPT (sound, ground giving way)
61-4	O/M	*dumm*-duh-duh-duh-DUHMMMM (*Dragnet* refrain: sound and depiction, heavy desolate feeling)
62-5	O/M	gasp (sound)
63-1	O/M	gRRCHH (movement, suddenly getting up)
63-2	O/M	ha ha ha
63-3	O/M	KOFF KOFF (depiction and sound)
	O/M	kwich
63-4	O/M	gGRPP (depiction, tying off her arm)
63-5	O/M (white)	pshhhht (depiction, intravenous injection of hard drugs)
	O/M (black)	*uhhhh* (depiction)
63-5	O/M (black)	*uhhhh* (depiction)
64-3	O/M	sPAZz sPAZZ (depiction, violent shaking)
64-3	O/M	WHEEZE (sound)
	O/M	WHEEEZE (sound)
64-4	O/M	flutter (depiction, faltering)
	O/M	wbbl (depiction)
64-5	O/M	DRGgg DRGGG drrGGG (depiction, somebody dragging themselves on the floor)
65-1	O/M	thmp (sound, door closing)
65-2	O/M	shhlp (sound, rustling paper)
65-5	O/M (white)	WOOOOooo0000 (sound, siren)
	O/M	(black, below white) EEEE EEEE EEEE EEEE (different siren)
	O/M (white)	WOOOOoooo0000 (sound, siren)
	O/M	(black, below white) EEEE EEEE EEEE EEEE (different siren)
	O/M	(right of tower) krakkl (sound of flames)
	O/M	(right of tower) krakkkl (sound of flames)
	O/M	(left of tower) kaBOOOOM (sound, explosion)
66-2	O/M (black)	rrROARrr (sound)
66-2	O/M (white)	*YAAAAAA* (mob roar)
66-3	O/M	rrROARrr (sound)
	O/M	ThUDD THuD ThUDD THuD ThUDD (sound, somebody running, very noisily)
66-4	O/M (black)	shmp (movement, body posture)
	O/M (white)	kSCHAK (sound, gun being jostled about in hand)
	O/M (black)	klaCHAK (sound, guns being loaded)
67-1	O/M	*YAAAAA* (sound)
67-1	O/M	ThUDD THuD ThUDD THuD ThUDD (sound, somebody running, very noisily)
67-2	O/M	*yaaaa* (sound)
67-4	O/M	DASH (depiction)
68-1	O/M	rrrrRUFF! RUFF! RUFF! (sound, Mince barking)
68-1	O/M	THMPA THMPA THMPA THMPA (sound, somebody running, very noisily)
68-3	O/M (white)	ThUDD THuD ThUDD THuD ThUDD (sound, somebody running, very noisily)
68-4	O/M	THMPa THMPa THMPa THMPa (sound, somebody running, noisy)
69-2	O/M	THWAMM (sound, vibrating pole thrust into ground)
69-3	O/M	SHWOOOM (movement, rapid dramatic movement)
70-1	O/M (white)	THWOK (sound)
	O/M (black)	crunch (depiction, Mince getting squashed)
	O/M	gwnch (movement, suddenly getting up)
70-3	O/M (tone)	vvvRRRMMMM (sound, truck)
	O/M	krakklkl krrrkll (sound, fire raging)
	O/M	kTHUNK kTHMP (sound, bumps that the truck is making)
71-1	O/M	SHLUMP (depiction and movement, Mince's head)
	O/M	kTHUNK kTHMP (sound, bumps that the truck is making)
	O/M	klank klunk (something metallic being shook by the truck's motion)
71-2	O/M	vrrrrrmmmmm (sound, truck)
71-3	O/M	aoooHOWWWWLLL (sound, mournful dog's howl)
72-2	O/M	shkk shkkk (sound, shaking)
72-6	O/M	kANg kANg kANg (sound, metallic stair climbing)
73-1	O/M	wheeze (sound)
73-2	O/M	kANg kANg (sound, metallic)
73-6	O/M	klack klack (sound, walking on a hard surface)
74-2	O/M	kTHMP (sound, door closing)
74-3	O/M	wwoooooooo (depiction, cold, "haunted" wind blowing through)
75-2	O/M	FSHH (depiction, light illumination)
	O/M	vrrrMMMMM (sound, car)
75-3	O/M	RRRMMMMM (sound, car)
75-4	O/M	tremble tremble (depiction)
76-4	O/M	JOLT (depiction)
76-5	O/M	lub-DUP lub-DUP (sound, panicked heartbeat)
76-6	O/M	woooooooo (depiction, a cold wind in the night)
77-1	O/M	whiiih-h-h-h-nny! (sound, horse's neigh)
77-2	O/M	tink (depiction and movement, reacting to stimuli)
77-3	O/M	Hyap! Hyyyap! (sound, cute barking)
77-4	O/M	krrrch krrrchh (sound, abrasive drag, shoes crunching on gravel)
77-7	O/M	neigh? (sound, horse)
78-1	O/M	whiiinny (sound, horse's neigh)
78-2	O/M	kLaplaLup kLaplaLup (sound, horse's hooves, running)
78-3	O/M	kLaplaLup kLaplaLup (sound, horse's hooves, running)
78-4	O/M	*twing* (sound, arrows being shot)
	O/M	*twing* (sound, arrows being shot)
	O/M	kREEEK (sound, bowstring going taut)
	O/M	THWOOSH (sound, arrows being shot)
78-5	O/M	kLaplaLup kLaplaLup (sound, horse's hooves, running)
79-1	O/M	kLaplaLup kLaplaLup (sound, horse's hooves, running)
79-4	O/M	ch-chik (sound and depiction, lots of loose small objects, pills)
79-5	O/M	glug (sound)
80-1	O/M	kCHING thik (sound, light cord)
80-2	O/M	fwump (depiction, hitting the sack)
81-2	O/M	chink tink (sound and depiction, lots of loose small objects)
81-5	O/M	kthmp (sound, getting up)
	O/M	thhCHAKK thhCHAKK thhCHAKK (sound and depiction, moving things about)
82-3	O/M	kCHAK (sound, opening small metal flap)
83-2	O/M	wobbl wobbl (depiction, faltering about, dozing off)
	O/M	*zzzzzz*
	O/M	wobbl wobbl (depiction, faltering about, dozing off)
83-3	O/M	(upper section first) kTHUDD (sound)
	O/M	THWNCH (sound and depiction, a jabbing motion)
	O/M	kTHWAK (sound)
	O/M	CRUNCH (sound, crunching)
	O/M	KRAKK (sound, more pain)
	O/M	zzzzzzzz
	O/M	weeeee
85-1	O/M	wheeze wheeze

GUIDE TO *EXCEL SAGA* 01'S SOUND EFFECTS!

85-2 O/M s-swing (depiction, that cord again)
85-3 O/M yank (depiction)
O/M k-CHUNGG! (depiction, the floor opening up)
85-6 O/M FSST (movement, arm)
O/M wheeze wheeze
86-4 O/M krrrSPLOOOSH
86-5 O/M wupPLAsh (sound, splashing about in water)
O/M THraPLaSHH (sound, splashing about in water)
O/M (white) HAKK (sound, really bloody cough)
O/M (small, below white) splut (sound, something being cough up and splashing)
86-5 O/M wupPLAsh (sound, splashing about in water)
86-5 O/M GEHHHKKK (sound, another chunky cough)
O/M YIIIIKES
O/M (small) blublublub (sound, drowning sound like)
87-2 O/M flap (sound, rustling paper)
89-1 O/M CHRRP CHRRP (sound, insects)
89-5 O/M JOLT (depiction, jolting)
90-2 O/M shmmrr shhmmr shhmmrr (depiction, wavy heat)
90-3 O/M shwmp (sound, getting up)
O/M fwich (sound, flinching)
90-4 O/M k-*runchh* (sound, something crunching, soft)
90-5 O/M THMP THMP (sound, somebody running)
90-6 O/M kTMP kTMP (sound, somebody rushing about)
91-1 O/M (white) sHplashh (sound, water being poured)
O/M (black) *fssshh* (sound, the noise water makes when hitting a very hot object)
91-2 O/M SSSSSSSS (sound, steam)
O/M drrbbl drrnnl (depiction)
91-3 O/M fSSShh sssHHH (sound, steam)
O/M chrrrp chrrrrrp (sound, insects)
91-5 O/M shplip (sound, water sound)
91-6 O/M shprsh plrshh (sound, cutting through water, weak)
92-1 O/M shplsh (sound, water sound)
O/M PLOIPP PLOIPP (sound, water dripping)
92-4 O/M shak (sound, opening curtains)
92-5 O/M *MOST RESOLUTE* [the words as sound FX: Hyatt is most resolute on this particular point]
93-1 O/M *diiinnnggg* (sound, cooking timer ing)
93-2 O/M shhllp (depiction, slippery texture and/or smoothness)
93-3 O/M hhhrurrrrkkkk (depiction, reeling from strong sensation)
93-3 O/M *SHHLLRRP* (depiction, slippery texture and/or smoothness)
93-4 O/M DA-DA-*DAAAA!* (depiction, dramatic reinforcement)
94-5 O/M urrgk (depiction, exasperation)
95-1 O/M SSSHHHhhhheeee (sound, losing steam)
95-2 O/M (lower) *sshhhh*... (sound, steam)
O/M (left and right of Excel) fidget fidget (depiction)
95-3 O/M kkkkrrEEEE kkkrrEEEE (sound, cicadas)
95-5 O/M ssssss (sound, steam)
95-6 O/M BANG! (sound)
O/M gGGRRK (sound, something grinding)
96-1 O/M chCHIIIINGG(depiction, the sound of money)
O/M klaklaklala*klak* (sound, coin slowing coming to a stop)
96-6 FX paTINK (depiction and movement, reacting to stimuli)
97-1 O/M waddle waddle (movement)
97-2 O/M *whine whine* (sound)
97-4 O/M *DING-DONGG* (sound)
98-2 O/M nod (movement)
O/M nod (movement
98-3 O/M kKREEEK (door opening)
99-2 O/M DRRGgg drrGGGG (depiction, dragging)
O/M kkkkrrEEEE kkkkrrEEEE kkkkrrEEEE (sound, cicadas)
99-3 O/M smfff smffff (depiction)
99-5 O/M BROILLL BROILLLL BROILLLL (depiction)
99-6 O/M GASP! (sound)
100-1 O/M *BZZZZ BZZZZZ* (sound and depiction, a jabbing at the doorbell)
100-2 O/M BAM BAMM
100-2 O/M BAM BAMM
100-3 O/M kkCHAK (sound and depiction, preparing fire extinguisher)
100-4 O/M (above) *thmp*
O/M (bellow) KREEEK
100-5 O/M FWOOM (depiction, blast of hot air)
100-6 O/M (white) POP! (depiction, coming from nowhere)
O/M (black) sszzzll ssszzll sssszzzl ssszzzll (depiction)
101-1 O/M BROIL BRAISE (depiction)
O/M SIMMER (depiction)
O/M POACH FRY (depiction)
101-3 O/M (large) ssSHING (depiction and movement, showing off something)
O/M (small, bellow nose) smmfff
101-4 O/M k-klik (sound, mechanical)
101-5 O/M Oh...YEAH! (depiction and dialog)
102-1 O/M (tone) ffffSPOOOOSH (depiction and sound, fire extinguisher going off)
O/M (black) PPLLLSHHHH (depiction and sound, something body getting smothered)
102-1 O/M flutter flutter (movement)
102-2 O/M THAK! (sound, dry hard hit)
O/M kTHUD
O/M BANG
O/M fffshhhh... (depiction, quiet (cessation of noise))
102-3 O/M glug
103-1 O/M THBFFFFT (sound, spurting out)
103-3 O/M kkkkrrEEEE kkkkrrEEEE kkkkrrEEEE (sound, cicadas)
O/M ssshhhhh
103-5 O/M klakkaklakkaklakkaklakka (sound and depiction, lots and lots of loose small objects, pills)
103-6 O/M GLUG (sound)
104-4 O/M chakchak (sound and depiction, lots of loose small objects, pills)
105-1 O/M GASP (sound, Excel gasping)
105-5 O/M ffht ffhtt (depiction, walking, somewhat deliberately, like a child)
105-6 O/M klaCHANK (sound, metallic)
106-3 O/M klang (sound)
106-4 O/M k-thump (sound, door closing)
106-6 O/M toast (depiction)
106-6 O/M sear (depiction)
107-1 O/M ding-dong (sound)
107-2 O/M ding-dong (sound)
107-3 O/M kLACHK (sound, mechanical)
108-4 O/M SLAMMM (sound)
109-1 O/M (below) rrROARrr!! (depiction and sound—hungry as a lion)
O/M (black) twirl twirl (movement, twirling)
O/M rsttl rsttl (sound, opening paper packaging)
109-4 O/M *one...two...*
O/M Heh (sound, dialog)
110-3 O/M wwwoooooo (depiction, cold wind blowing through)
110-4 O/M wwweeeeoooo (depiction, cold wind blowing through)
110-5 O/M kANg kANg kANg (sound, metallic)
O/M purrr*PREEEEEET* (sound, tofu seller horn)
113-2 O/M YEAH!
113-4 O/M vMmmmm (sound and depiction, Il Palazzo slowly entering, illuminated)
114-1 O/M yank (depiction)
O/M Aaaagh (sound, dialog)
O/M kPLASHhh (sound, water)
114-2 O/M sPLAsh (sound, water)
O/M zplaSH (sound, water)
O/M wupPLAsh (sound, splashing about in water)

Guide to *Excel Saga* 01's Sound Effects!

114-3	0/M	plaCHWAP (sound of grabbing the lip of a pool getting out—if you can think of a better one, please go ahead)
115-1	0/M	phTHWIP (depiction, papers entering into panel and stopping movement)
115-2	0/M	FWUMPP FWUMPP (sound, clothing being flapped about)
115-3	0/M	fidget fidget fidget (depiction, anxiously getting dressed while listening to Il Palazzo)
115-4	0/M	ssSHING (depiction and movement, going into pose)
	0/M	tWONGG (depiction and movement, holding pose after movement)
116-1	0/M	chirp (sound, repeat as much as will fit into area)
116-4	0/M	phFWAP (depiction, papers entering into panel and stopping movement)
117-3	0/M	huff puff wheeze wheeze (sound)
118-2	0/M	hmph hhhrffff (sound)
118-3	0/M	grik (depiction, fastening something tight or closing a grip on something)
	0/M	ggrrppkk (depiction)
118-4	0/M	ggrrppp (depiction)
	0/M	ggrrppp (depiction)
118-5	0/M	grpp (depiction)
	0/M	ggrpp (depiction)
	0/M	ggripppkk (depiction)
	0/M	GRIK (depiction)
119-1	0/M	pfffTHWUMP (depiction, combination of pfft (light toss) and THWUMP (clothing snapping out against side of apartment))
119-2	0/M	skkrrrpp skkrrpp skrrrpp (dragging sound)
119-5	0/M	GRPP (depiction)
	0/M	wooo000ooo
123-3	0/M	gasp! (depiction)
123-4	0/M	ssSHING (depiction and movement, going into pose)
124-2	0/M	gasp! (depiction)
124-6	0/M	DASH (movement)
125-1	0/M	thTHMP thTHMP (depiction, walking, somewhat wobblingly and uncertain, like a young child)
126-2	0/M	kkRACKK (sound, components being dropped)
126-4	0/M	skkKKRP skkKKRPP (sound, heavy dragging him off, heels dug in)
126-5	0/M	kreek kreek [squeaky wheels of Excel's cart]
	0/M	skkKRRP skKRRP skKKRRP (sound)
126-6	0/M	kreek kreek kreek (sound)
127-1	0/M	wheeze wheeze wheeze (sound)
127-4	0/M	sSHINGg (depiction)
128-3	0/M	RSSTLL RSSTL (depiction)
128-6	0/M	SHINGg (depiction and sound, Excel making a "zeroing in" sound out loud)
129-1	0/M	kthmp... (depiction, causally sticking glass in place)
	0/M	sssssss (sound)
129-4	0/M	rsstl rsstl (sound)
	0/M	klaPOP (sound, opening a wood box)
129-8	0/M	one..two..*three!* [lifting up cart]
129-9	0/M	twirl (movement)
130-1	0/M	SnaPP KrackLe (sound)
130-3	0/M	wHOOMF krkkl (sound, reinforcement of fire's power)
131-1	0/M	DASH (depiction and movement)
131-2	0/M	(kana, white, far upper and lower right) ffWHAPP ffWHAPP (movement, flapping clothing—only fanning the flames)
	0/M	(hiragana, white, middle) heeYAHH! heeYAA! heeYAAH! (sound, Excel dialog)
	0/M	(kana, white, left) ffhhhWHAPP (movement, flapping clothing)
	0/M	(kana, black, far left) ffROAr krkkl rrRoaRR (flames, growing)
131-3	0/M	*HAHH* oooh ooooh *HAHH HAHH* (wheezing sound)
131-3	0/M	KKKRRRRRRR (sound of roaring flames)
131-5	0/M	tmp (depiction)
	0/M	splOOSHH (sound, liquid inside)
132-1	0/M (large)	FHOOOOMP (sound, gas igniting)
	0/M (small)	plishhh (sound, liquid hitting something)
132-2	0/M	*smolder* (sound and depiction)
	0/M	(far left) RROARR (sound, fire bursting out)
132-4	0/M	fWHOOMP KKRRRR (sound, reinforcement of fire's power)
133-1	0/M	RRRRRRR (sound, reinforcement of fire's power)
133-2	0/M	KRKKL ROARRR (sound, fire bursting out)
133-4	0/M	kaZING! (depiction and movement, going into pose, extra dramatic)
133-5	0/M (upper)	woooOOOO woooOOOO (Excel making "fire truck" siren noise)
	0/M (lower)	kkREEEK kkkREEEK (sound, cart pulling sounds)
133-6	0/M (upper)	wooooo00000 (sound, Excel's siren imitation)
	0/M (middle)	klang klang klang (sound, Excel making bell noises)
	0/M (lower)	veep! voooop! (sound, Excel making radio squawking noises)
133-6	0/M (furthest bottom)	kkkREEK kkkREEK kkkREEK kkkREEK (sound, cart pulling sounds)
137-4	0/M	wheeze (sound)
	0/M	wheeeeeze (sound)
139-2	0/M	kTNK (sound, shoes sounds)
139-3	0/M	(near Excel's feet) pffTAP pffTAP (sound, light tapping sounds, adjusting her feet in her shoes)
	0/M	(near Hyatt's face) cughh cough (sound)
139-4	0/M	KOFF (sound)
139-5	0/M	SLAMM! (sound)
141-1	0/M	fwik (sound, rustling paper)
141-2	0/M	Ha ha ha (dialog)
141-5	0/M	YANK (movement)
	0/M	kERchUNK (sound, trap door opening)
143-3	0/M	UMMM... (dialog)
144-1	0/M	wheeze huff puff hufff (sounds)
144-2	0/M	couff huff KOFF (sounds)
144-3	0/M	pitter pitter (sound, walking)
145-2	0/M	paTINK (depiction and movement, reacting to stimuli)
145-3	0/M	wheeze huff (sounds)
145-4	0/M	couff huff cough huff (sounds)
145-5	0/M	klench (depiction)
	0/M	(upper left) flinch (depiction)
145-6	0/M	huff wheeze (sounds)
145-7	0/M	whiiiiine (sound, Mince is worried about poor Hyatt)
146-1	0/M	wheeze hufff (sound)
	0/M	gGRIP (depiction)
	0/M	THRASH KICK JERK FLAIL (sound and depiction, Mince's desperate trying to break free)
146-2	0/M	whhhhooowwwwlll!!! (sound, loud scream like whine)
	0/M	skkkRAK (sound, rumbling opening sound)
146-3	0/M	(next to Sumiyoshi's foot) creeeaak (sound)
	0/M	huff wheeze puff (sounds)
146-4	0/M	wheeze wheeezz (sounds)
	0/M	rsstl rsstl (sounds)
	0/M	(below Watanabe) cuFF koff (sounds)
147-1	0/M	nod (depiction)
	0/M	wheeze (sound)
147-2	0/M	wheeze (sound)
147-3	0/M	KOFF (sound)
147-4	0/M	GRAPP (grabbing depiction)
147-4	0/M	*cough* (sound)
147-5	0/M	COUGH KAUFF (sound)
147-6	0/M	hhhWHEEZE hhhWHEEZE (sound)
148-1	0/M	skkrrKKTt (sound, rumbling opening sound)
148-2	0/M	kTHMP (sound, closing sliding door)

GUIDE TO *EXCEL SAGA* 01'S SOUND EFFECTS!

148-2	FX	KOFF (sound)
148-3	FX	cough (sound)
	FX	cough (sound)
148-4	FX	kCHAK (sound, door knob turning)
	FX	fffWHMP (sound, getting up quickly)
148-5	FX	AWWHHKK HAKKK HAWWKK (sounds)
149-3	FX	zssZSHING (depiction and movement, going into pose)
	FX	flinch (alarmed reaction)
150-2	FX	root (digging in pocket)
150-3	FX	pattpattpattpattpattpatt (sound and depiction, patting down her pockets for her money packet in fast succession)
151-2	FX	SHOOF (depiction and movement)
	FX	flinch (alarmed reaction)
	FX	flinch (alarmed reaction)
152-2	FX	plod plod (depiction and movement, walking with no energy)
152-5	FX	tmpa tmpa (depiction, walking deliberately)
	FX	twirl (movement)
152-6	FX	GASP (depiction)
152-7	FX	nod (movement)
	FX	wwwooOOOSH (movement)
153-1	FX	POOF (hi-speed arrival)
	FX	sskkkRAKK (rumbling opening sound of slide door)
153-6	FX	wwww00000oooooo (depiction, cold wind blowing through)
154-2	FX	kThump (sound, door closing)
154-4	FX	fwnch (movement, coming free from hand)
154-6	FX	Let's see (sound, dialog)
155-6	FX	hugg (depiction)
155-7	FX	kyueen? kyueen? (sound, cute whine)
155-8	FX	twitch (movement)
156-1	FX	fhhWUMP (movement)
156-2	FX	lubDUP lubDUP lubDUP lubDUP (sound, heart beat)
156-4	FX	Oh, *my*....... (sound, dialog)
156-5	FX	bubble toil trouble (sound, boiling, popping, steaming)
156-5	FX	wheeeezze (sound)
156-5	FX	wheeezzze (sound)
157-1	FX	kCHAnk SHINGG (sound, bells and etc.)
157-2	FX	klaPOWPOWPOWPOW! (sound of holiday crackers going off)
157-4	FX	kCHAnk SHINGG (sound, bells and etc.)
157-5	FX	kCHANK (sound, bells and etc.)
160-3	FX	hahhh hahhh (sound)
160-4	FX	chatter chatter (depiction)
	FX	(on Excel's head) Oh, *man*...
161-1	FX	DDDRRRMMM (sound, drum flourish)
161-2	FX	fWUMP (Desslok-like settling of the cape)
162-5	FX	Umph! Umph! (sound, dialog)
163-1	FX	sshWIP shWPP (movement, looking about)
163-5	FX	zssZSHING (depiction and movement, going into pose)
164-1	FX	awe (depiction, in awe with Il Palazzo said)
164-4	FX	sSHingG (depiction and movement, going into pose)
164-4	FX	*K-SHANG* (depiction and movement, going into pose, extra dramatic)
	FX	shSHING (depiction and movement, going into pose)
165-1	FX	(sound, cute phone ring)
165-2	FX	diddle-dee-dee (sound, cell phone ring—note: new one from Mission 1)
	FX	diddley-dee-dee-dee (sound, cell phone ring)
165-3	FX	dee-dee-diddley-dee (sound, cell phone ring)
165-4	FX	beBEEP (sound, beeping sound made as button is pressed to connect the phone)
165-8	FX	phew! (sound, dialog)
166-1	FX (black, right)	gGRUGHH gGRUGHH (sound, crocodile sounds, bark like)
	FX (tone)	*CROCODILES—! CROCODILES—!* (sound, dialog)
	FX (black, left)	*ggGRAAAAa* (sound, crocodile, threatening exhale)
167-4	FX	shddr shvvr shiver (shivering—not from fear but impending physical collapse)
167-5	FX	*rsstl* (sound)
168-4	FX	awwwHAKK (sound, bloody spewing cough)
168-5	FX	SPLUSHT (sound and movement, blood splashing)
168-6	FX	THMP-A THMP-A THMP-A THMP-A (sound, forceful walking away)
169-4	FX	kCHAnk kCHAnk kCHANK (bottles rustling in bag)
169-5	FX	(lower right) rustle (sound)
	FX	sSHingG (depiction and movement, going into pose)
170-2	FX	LEAN (depiction, edging ever closer toward someone)
170-4	FX	Ha ha ha ha (sound, dialog, dry laughter)
171-3	FX	kBlam BLAM RATATATAT (sound, gunfight)
171-4	FX	paTING klaPING SPANG kPING (sound, bullets ricochet off Iwata)
171-5	FX	kKLAk CLANK kKLAk kKLAk CLANK kKLAk (clashing swords)
172-2	FX	rustle (sound)
172-5	FX	kCHAnk (sound, change)
173-3	FX	GASP (depiction)
174-1	FX	vvveeeEEEEEE vvvvEEEEE (sound, approaching sound of sirens)
174-2	FX	kTHMP (sound, door closing)
	FX	TMP TMP TMP (sound, running)
	FX	rhubarb rhubarb rhubarb (depiction, crowd murmuring about)
174-3	FX	kICHANK (sound, mechanical)
	FX	KLANK (sound, mechanical)
174-4	FX	(small, near middle of panel) murmur murmur (depiction, crowd murmuring about)
	FX	(bottom) kCHANK (sound, mechanical)
174-5	FX	buhWWeeEEEE (sound, siren starting up)
174-6	FX	VEEP VOOP VEEP VOOP (sound, electronic horns)
	FX	vvvRRRMMM (sound, driving away)
175-4	FX	THAK THAK THAK (sound, forceful walking)
175-5	FX	kTHAK kTHAK kTHAK kTHAK kTHAK kTHAK (sound, forceful walking)
176-1	FX	THAK THAK (sound, forceful walking)
176-2	FX	THAK THAK (sound, forceful walking)
176-3	FX	kWHAMM (sound, door)
176-5	FX	harumph! (depiction, excited exhale through nose)
177-4	FX	(depiction, above head) YOU CAN'T SEE IT BUT HIS EYES ARE WIDENING
178-1	FX	kchak (sound, mechanical, opening door)
178-2	FX	sSHingG! (depiction and movement, going into pose)
179-2	FX	sob (sound, dialog)
179-3	FX	kRAck (sound of Dr. Iwata getting elbowed)
180-1	FX	(behind Excel) *HUH !? WHAT THE HELL!?*
	FX	THMP THMP THMP (movement, walking fast)
180-4	FX	Waaa ha ha ha!
180-5	FX	glub glub blub blublubbb (sound, pouring)
181-3	FX	SIGH (depiction and sound)
182-1	FX	Humph! (sound, dialog)
182-2	FX	SHMP (depiction and movement, going into pose)
	FX	HAW HAW HAW (sound, dialog)
	FX	What a maroon! (sound, dialog)
183-4	FX	heh hee-hee (sound, dialog)
184-6	FX	GAZE (depiction)
184-7	FX	kTHMP (sound, door)
	FX	OBSERVE
186-1	FX	vvvvvMMMMM (depiction, rising presence)
186-4	FX	VVVVMMMMM (depiction, dramatic forcefulness)
188-2	FX	shove (depiction, charging ever closer toward someone)
188-4	FX	SHOCK! (depiction)
	FX	tmp tmp tmp tmp (sound, somebody running, noisy)
188-7	FX	klaklaklaklak (sound, pushing buttons)
188-8	FX	klaklaklaklak (sound, pushing buttons)
188-9	FX	chirp chirp (sound, birds)
189-1	FX	ssSHING (depiction and movement, going into pose)
189-3	FX	DASH! (movement)

GUIDE TO *EXCEL SAGA* 01'S SOUND EFFECTS!

FOOTNOTES

Written by translator Dan Kanemitsu
With additions by editor Carl Gustav Horn

11-1: The technical translation of their name is "Ideology Realization Organization *Across*." The editor askes you to compare ACROSS's HQ with that of Fukuoka's actual ACROS (Asian CrossRoads Over the Sea) building: http://www.acros.or.jp/english/04_acros. html I suppose this is equivalent to an organization trying to take over New York City calling itself "Javits" or one trying to conquer San Francisco, "Moscone."

23-2-1: This is an excerpt from the poetry of famous Japanese poet, Ozaki Hosai (1885-1926). Stone Bridge Press, already known for books on anime and manga, publishes Ozaki in translation:
http://www.stonebridge.com/bigsky/bigsky.html

23-4: The original Japanese pun here was between two words said the same but with different kanji readings: *seifuku*, "uniform," and *seifuku*, "conquest."

34-1-1: "Dozaemon" is a proper noun, but is more commonly used to refer to dead bodies floating in water. Dozaemon was a very fat Sumo wrestler, so fat that people started to use his name to refer to the ballooned-up waterborne bodies, and eventually, his name came to represent all waterborne dead bodies. The Edo period was from 1603-1868; you know, like in *Lone Wolf and Cub*.

38-5: In the Japanese text, there is a distinction of what kind of flood. In Japan, how much a house has submerged is a way of describing the magnitude of a floods. Since Japanese homes rarely have basements, most floors of houses are elevated off the ground. When the water level is below the floor, it is referred to as *yukashita shinsui*, "below floor water seepage" but when the water level goes above the floor, it is referred to as *yukaue shinsu*, "above floor water seepage." Original text "This is more like a flood than a some above floor water seepage."

39-2: In the original, Excel refers not to the Col., but to the keroyon frog mascot seen in front of many pharmacies in Japan. But since of the two floating figures, the plastic fried chicken magnate is more familiar to Americans, the editor decided to switch the object of her comment.

39-5 In the original text, the joke works by using two different readings of the same kanji combination: seibutsu, "living thing," and namamono, "uncooked food".

53-1-2 The text below the panel is an obscure reference that only the people who actually worked on the manga are said to understand.

54-2: The Japanese name means "Maritime Safety Agency," but the official government translation in English is "Japan Coast Guard." More Orwellian is the difference between the official translation, "Immigration Bureau," which is called in Japanese the "Border Control Bureau."

67-2: Original theme, "The Song Of The Defenders." This is a reference based on a Japanese movie, *Hill 203*. The movie depicts the futile but courageous charge of Japanese troops in the Russo-Japanese War. Japanese soldiers were slaughtered trying to take this hill from the Tzarist Russian troops. "The Charge Of The Light Brigade" seemed to the editor a change very true in spirit to the original, but one more likely to make the joke work for Western readers.

68-1-4: Original text used the name, Pochi, which is a generic dog name in Japan, and the heroine of Gainax's computer game *Animal Magnetism: Pochi no Daisuki*, for which Tomoko Saito did the character designs. You see people cos-playing as Pochi these days.

92-5-1: The original text included a reference to dried seaweed, commonly used for various types of Japanese cooking, as well as to the lotus seed, which is famous in Asia for being very resilient, enough that it can be dried and left out in the open for hundreds of years, but then return it into wet dirt, and it can sprout. The editor felt a reference to "sea monkeys," recently revived by *South Park*, would make the joke work better; also, sea monkeys have a long and proud association with comics in America.

Guide to *Excel Saga* 01's Sound Effects!

97-5: NHK is the Japanese version of the BBC. Each year, these stations "request" that the individual viewer "faithfully carryout the duty as a viewer and a citizen" and pay a certain fee each year. The basic system is you pay a certain amount for each household. If you don't have a TV, you don't have to pay. This later part will come clear in the next episode.

102-2-2: *Ohigan* or *higan*, is the time of the year in Japan when the dead are thought to return to their houses and stay with their remaining relatives for a while. This usually takes place in mid-August.

105-3-2: The original Japanese pun here was between two words said the same but with different kanji readings: *eiyo*, "glory," and *eiyo*, "nutrition."

105-7-3: As above; the pun was between *shoumi*, "actual weight," and *shoumi*, "date to be eaten by." The editor came up with the English version in this case.

116: Also known as the Camel Cricket. Japanese name *kamado uma*. Common name: *Benjyokorogi* (Bathroom Cricket). Full scientific name of Cave Cricket *Arthorpod Insecta Orthoptera Saltatoria Ceuthophilus*.

120-1: Original line was a pun on *chikush(o)* as in livestock animal and *chikush(o)* as in the explicative, i.e. Damn it! I think this English phrasing captures the dual nuance of the original text fairly well.

122-3-1: Sumiyoshi speaks in the original manga in the distict Okayama-area accent of Japan. Whereas the editor, working on *Neon Genesis Evangelion*, decided to render Toji's Kansai accent as a sort of Brooklynese (on the advice of a person from Kansai who had lived in New York City), the translator of *Excel Saga* looks to regional equivalents in Britain as opposed to the United States. He suggested a "Northern England" feel for Okayama; the editor then rendered Sumiyoshi's dialogue according to Tyneside's silver-tongued cavalier in the great U.K. magazine *Viz* (no relation to VIZ, LLC). As you will see, though, Sumiyoshi, even if he does speak with the tongue of Sid the Sexist and Biffa Bacon, is himself a nice, decent guy. Note that although the story takes place in Fukuoka prefecture, nearly every one in *Excel Saga* talks in a standard Tokyo dialect with some local Fukuoka sayings sneaking in, here and then.

129-3: A 16 bit computer for children built by Tomy of Japan, first introduced in 1982 as the *Pyu~ta* but later exported to the US as the Tomy Tutor. Featured the Texas Instrument's 16 bit TMS9995 CPU, Basic ROM, game cartridge interface system, and standard audio tape save function. Very obscure and short lived system that is fondly remembered by some.

129-5: Bad pun. Original *Mariko yakedo*. The first part barely rhythms with the last part.

133-6: *Hansho* is a bronze bell that was rung in times of emergency. There is no equivalent in the US (since church bells are rarely rung in case of emergencies any more, I'm not sure if there is any way around this.)

135-1-2: The editor thinks this description of the monitor is technically inaccurate on purpose. Feel free to write in on this one.

137-3-1: Japan has a national health plan, so Excel is referring to her government benefits. But don't let that fool *you* into supporting replacing the generous, compassionate, bureaucracy-free care you receive from your private HMO with another government agency!

148-5-2: *Tamagozake* (egg and sake) is considered to be an effective cold remedy by some. It's a traditional/jock thing that gets passed down from generation to generation. More of a joke than anything else.

175-5-1: This *Blackjack*-lookin' quack is actually Norikuni Iwata's cousin, Dr. Sekifumi Iwata. For the purposes of this translation, Sekifumi will be referred to as Dr. Iwata. There are two more Iwatas who will show up later in *Excel Saga*.

184-6-1: Classic subversive narrative device. By employing a Chinese character with a specific meaning as an onomatopoeia, it produces an chuckle for its inappropriateness and bold non-diegetic delivery. Yeah!